Growing Up in a One-Parent Family

Growing up in a one-parent family: a long-term study of child development

Elsa Ferri

NFER Publishing Company Ltd

Published by the NFER Publishing Company Ltd.,
2 Jennings Buildings, Thames Avenue,
Windsor, Berks. SL4 1QS
Registered Office: The Mere, Upton Park, Slough, Berks. SL1 2DQ
First published 1976
© National Children's Bureau
ISBN 0 85633 087 6

Typeset by Jubal Multiwrite Ltd.,
66 Loampit Vale, London SE13 7SN
Printed in Great Britain by
Staples Printers Ltd., Rochester, Kent

Cover designed by Ken Arlotte

Distributed in the USA by Humanities Press Inc.,
Hilary House-Fernhill House, Atlantic Highlands,
New Jersey 07716 USA.

ACKNOWLEDGMENTS

My thanks are due to the Department of Health and Social Security for providing the financial support which made this study possible.

I also gratefully acknowledge the help received from various members of the Bureau staff, past and present. In particular I wish to thank Janet Birch for her able work as research assistant to the project throughout its duration; Rachel Peto for her statistical advice and for undertaking the statistical analyses, and Felicity Willetts, who was responsible for processing the data.

I am also grateful to Peter Wedge for his helpful advice and comments at various stages of the project, and to other colleagues who gave their time to offer constructive criticism of the manuscript, notably Dr Mia Kellmer Pringle, Harvey Goldstein, Hilary Robinson, Lydia Lambert and Ken Fogelman.

The research is based on material collected for the National Child Development Study, and I should finally like to express my thanks to all those who were involved in the collection of this information: the teachers, doctors, health visitors, local authority staff — and, of course, the parents and children themselves.

Elsa Ferri

Contents

List of Tables in Appendix 2

Chapter One

The family in our society

'The problem of the single parent family is related to the fact that today society is dominated by the idea of the nuclear family'.

Benjamin Schlesinger (1966)

Nearly all of us have been closely involved from birth onwards in a complex network of family relationships. The part played by such relationships in virtually every sphere of the growing child's development is of unquestionable importance. However, the actual ways in which a family influences its individual members is an area which is not easily approached in an objective, scientific manner. Few other institutions are so dependent upon the emotional commitment of their members and consequently few institutions are so difficult to view from a standpoint of detached observation. The need for such an approach to the family is not one which receives wide recognition: 'The fact that most adults are members of at least two families leads to the belief that all are experts on family life and that the findings related to the family are obvious and require little further investigation' (Heraud 1970).

Studies of the effects of the family on the development of individuals tend to focus on its failures rather than on its successes. Symptoms of delinquent or maladjusted behaviour are frequently the cue for a probing search for adverse family circumstances which might offer a causal explanation. Much less interest is aroused by the home background characteristics of individuals who display no behavioural problems.

The catalogue of potentially adverse family circumstances invariably contains a reference to the broken home. The 'anomalous' nature of the one-parent family makes it an obvious target for attack as a causal factor in numerous social and psychological ills, and often the search for explanatory factors goes no further.

That the one-parent family deviates *statistically* from the norm is unquestionable. However, the effects frequently attributed to it are, in many instances, based less on sound evidence than on the unspoken assumption that one parent cannot adequately perform a role which society allocates to two. Although it is frequently pointed out that living with both natural parents is no guarantee of a healthy home environment, it often appears to be taken for granted that the child cared for by only one parent will necessarily be deprived of certain essential features of a 'normal' home life. It is rarely spelled out, however, in what ways and to what extent the family life of one-parent children differs from that of children living with both parents, and even less often is an attempt made to assess the effects of any observed variations in specific areas of child development. It was the main aim of the research reported here to fill some of these gaps by studying a large, representative sample of children in one and two-parent families, comparing factors in their respective backgrounds and environments and relating these factors to their educational, social, and emotional development.

A study of one-parent families cannot begin however, without first taking a look at the characteristic features of what is the 'normal' family type in our present day society – i.e. the two-parent 'nuclear' family. Some writers (e.g. Laslett, 1972) have suggested that this, rather than the multi-generational, extended family has always been the norm in Western society. However, it is the characteristics, rather than the historical development, of the typical family unit which are of importance in the present study, since it is only by drawing a clear picture of the role and function of this 'normal' family that we can examine the ways in which the one-parent situation differs from the norm and assess the effects such differences might have on the lives of the individuals concerned.

The typical family unit in our complex, mobile industrial society consists of father, mother and their children, living in a state of greater geographical, economic and social independence from other relatives and kin than was common even a few decades ago. In recent years, some social commentators have seen this reduction of the family unit as reflecting a transfer of the family's functions in such areas as health care, education and the organization of leisure activities, to other, more specialized, agencies. Some (e.g. Wilson, 1962) go so far as to suggest that the death knell of the family as a social institution has already sounded, and that we are witnessing its gradual decline and decay.

Other writers strongly challenge this view, and claim that the family's function as 'the only social institution charged with transforming a biological organism into a human being' (Goode, 1964) remains as important as ever. However, changes have occurred in the *ways* in which this function is carried out. No longer is the child to be prepared to fill a position in society which is ascribed, clearly defined and unlikely to change. Today's fluid and diversified society needs adults equipped to act in a variety of often changing roles, for which the behaviour, values and attitudes of the parental generation may have little relevance. Such a society demands a more child-centred approach to child-rearing with attention focused on the social and psychological well-being of the developing child as well as on the nurturance of his talents and capacities. The role of the modern parent in this context was clearly summed up by Titmuss (1953):

> 'Society is in the process of making parenthood a highly self-conscious, self-regarding affair. In so doing it is adding heavily to the sense of personal responsibility among parents. Their tasks are much harder and involve more risks of failure when children have to be brought up as individual successes in a supposedly mobile, individualistic society rather than in a traditional and repetitive society. Bringing up children becomes less a matter of rule-of-thumb custom and tradition and more a matter of acquired knowledge and of expert advice. More decisions have to be made because there is so much more to be decided, and as the margin of felt responsibility extends, so does the scope for anxiety about one's children.'

Fletcher (1966) also points out that, rather than being stripped of its functions, more specialized demands are made on the family by a society which 'expects a responsible undertaking of far more social commitments'. The provision of state education for all children, for example, far from depriving the family of its educative function, has developed in such a way that the parents' co-operation and participation in the teaching/learning process is now regarded as a prerequisite to the child's optimal development. Similarly in the field of health, the growth of public health service provision has gone hand in hand with a rise in standards of care and hygiene which demand more, rather than less, of parents in terms of informed practice and preventive care.

In the small nuclear or 'conjugal' family the tasks of child-rearing fall much more exclusively on the child's parents than was the case when grandparents and other relatives were more readily available to share such responsibilities. How are these tasks allocated between the mother and the father in the modern family? An examination of the literature reveals that, while the role of the mother in providing a warm, secure, nurturing environment for the developing child has been well-documented, the position of the father in the family situation is much less clearly defined. Frequently the father's role appears to be confined to one of economic support and provision — as Nash (1965) points out he is regarded almost as a 'statistical appendage' to the family. Bowlby (1966), in fact, sees the father as 'of no direct importance to the young child but is of indirect value as an economic support and in his emotional support of the mother.' Other writers (e.g. Andry, 1966; Bronfenbrenner, 1970; Comfort, 1970;) have felt that the lack of attention paid to the role of the father bears little relation to its importance for the socialization of the child, and that more thought should be devoted to this aspect of family relationships. Pilling (in press) reviews recent research which shows fairly consistently the importance of the father's behaviour and interaction with the child for both cognitive and social/emotional development.

The question of how far parental roles overlap or remain distinct or 'segregated' is one which has drawn the attention of a number of writers on the family. In recent years, observers have noted a trend towards a greater degree of overlap between maternal and paternal roles; for example, Young and Willmott (1957) found that among working class families in Bethnal Green, domestic activities and child care could no longer be regarded as the province of the mother alone, and, in a later study (1973), describe the trend towards the 'symmetrical' family, in which husband and wife undertake parallel roles both in and out of the home. Bronfenbrenner (1961), in the United States, commented that 'the balance of power within the family has continued to shift, with fathers yielding parental authority to mothers and taking on some of the nurturant and affectional functions traditionally associated with the maternal role.' The Newsons (1970) found in their study that this trend had moved downwards through the social class scale, and that only in homes of unskilled workers were more 'traditional' family patterns still prevalent. In such families 'the father is more likely to be described by his wife as "stricter" than herself and accorded greater prestige as an authority figure. He is less likely to participate in story-telling and to share an interest with the seven-year-old.' Other writers (e.g. Bell and Vogel, 1968; Bott, 1959; Slater, 1960) have linked the degree of overlap or segregation between parental roles to the parents' relationships with other members of the family and the community. The less the couple form part of a close-knit network of relationships, the more likely are they to share domestic and child-rearing activities. Thus, the more the nuclear family lives in 'isolation' from the extended family, the greater the degree of sharing of activities between husband and wife.

The relative isolation of the nuclear family as an economically and socially independent unit is seen by some writers as producing strains and tensions less often found in an extended family system. Bowlby (1966) comments that 'as a result of this social fragmentation a far heavier responsibility for child care is placed on the father and mother than is the case in more primitive, close-knit communities'.

A further outcome of the isolated position of the nuclear family is seen in a heightening of emotional intensity between its members. Despert (1962) claims that 'inevitably there must develop within this family stripped to its fewest and most intimate relationships a compensating intensity in these relationships'. This intensity is seen by Goode (1964) as creating both the 'intimacy' and the 'fragility' of the modern conjugal family situation.

The characteristic features of the 'normal' family situation in our society may thus be summed up as follows. It is a small unit consisting of father, mother and their children. This unit and other members of the wider family are much less interdependent than was the case at an earlier period. In such a situation, the responsibilities of child-rearing are concentrated on the parents alone, responsibilities which have become increasingly complex and demanding in response to similar changes in the wider society. There has been a trend towards the merging of paternal and maternal roles in the child-rearing process, although the extent to which this occurs is related to other factors in the family situation, such as social class background and the family's relationships with kin and community. It has been suggested that another outcome of the relative 'isolation' of the nuclear family lies in the heightening of the emotional tension between its members, which renders their relationships more fragile and vulnerable.

What are the implications for the one-parent family of the foregoing discussion of the 'normal' family in our society?

Firstly, as the 'normal' family consists of two parents, the one-parent family is, by definition, deviant. The very fact of such deviance will have implications for the status of the one-parent family and for the treatment it receives. Sprey (1969) has pointed out that 'it is not a great leap from an infrequent, often ambiguous, status to a socially stigmatized one'. Other writers (e.g. Goode, 1964; Hansen and Hill, 1964; Schlesinger, 1966) have suggested that the degree to which the one-parent family elicits society's support or censure is related to the cause of the situation, with widow's families receiving the greatest sympathy and those of unmarried mothers being the focus of hostility. Thus, although the modern family has become an increasingly independent unit, it cannot be studied in isolation from the wider society, since it is in the context of that society that the family carries out its functions and receives, or is refused, support. The ambiguities of the one-parent family's status was summed up by Kriesberg (1970) when he wrote: 'Many of the difficulties faced by mothers and children in female-headed households are not inherent to that family structure. The difficulties in part stem from the expectations of others about what is a normal family, from the socially limited alternatives deemed appropriate for women, and the specificity of sex roles.'

The social position of a family headed by a lone parent is thus far from clearly defined. The relative isolation and independence of the 'nuclear family' from other family members means that, as Goode (1964) has pointed out, no kinship group is expected to be responsible for the care and support of members of families which are broken by death or marital breakdown. State agencies are obliged to provide basic material assistance to those in need (although there is evidence that this may be inadequate to guarantee the continuance of a one-parent family as an economic unit). However, no group or agency is generally expected to provide support for the lone parent in what we have described as the most demanding task of modern parenthood, namely to prepare children for participation in a complex and changing adult society.[1]

Even less clearly defined are society's expectations concerning the role the lone parent is to play. For example, the question of whether the parent should work or care full-time for the children of the family is one which may arouse considerable controversy — especially when the parent concerned is the father.

The remaining parent is faced with the task of attempting to take over singlehanded the role of the absent partner in addition to his or her own. To the extent that paternal and maternal roles had previously differed, this would seem to create a particular problem — especially where the two roles appear incompatible. For example, Marsden (1969), in a study of mothers as lone parents, reported that 'they found a conflict in trying to be the centre both of authority and affection for their children'. It is interesting to speculate whether the task would be more easily undertaken in families in which paternal and maternal roles had shown a high degree of overlap.

The relatively high level of emotional intensity seen by some writers as characterizing the modern 'nuclear' family would seem likely to be heightened even further by the loss of one of its members. Many case-workers have commented on the strains and conflicts in one-parent families resulting from the increased emotional dependence of the remaining parent and children.

---

1   The growth in recent years of self-help groups such as Gingerbread and Mothers in Action, and the extension of the role of the National Council for One-Parent Families (formerly the National Council for the Unmarried Mother and her Child), testify to the lack of needed support for one-parent families.

This brief consideration of the position of the one-parent family in our present day society would seem to point to a potential vulnerability and to considerable strains and difficulties attached to bringing up children in such a situation. So far, however, our discussion has remained theoretical and speculative. In the next chapter we shall look briefly at the findings of other investigations of the effects upon children's development of living in a one-parent family.

Chapter Two

How one-parent families affect
their children: a review of research

A considerable amount has been written about the effects upon children of living in a one-parent family. It is interesting to find that while, as mentioned in the previous chapter, discussion of parent-child relationships has concentrated largely on the role of the mother, in the case of the one-parent family attention has focused almost exclusively on situations where the *father* is the absent parent. Apart from investigations by Bowlby and others of the effects of maternal deprivation on very young children (which in fact mostly concern children experiencing *parental* deprivation and separation from home), studies of children in motherless families are conspicuous by their absence.

Much of the literature on one-parent families consists of theoretical and speculative writings or analyses of case histories of individuals receiving guidance or therapy. While providing valuable insight into the potential problems facing broken families, such material cannot be used to make general statements about the effects of one-parent situations. The studies which will be referred to here are those which have set out to assess the effects of such family circumstances in measurable areas of behaviour.

Two major difficulties are immediately encountered in evaluating the findings of studies of one-parent families. Firstly, the nature of the samples investigated varies widely. In some cases, for example, all types of broken family are included regardless of the cause of the situation, others look only at families broken by divorce or separation. Some investigations include children in 'ever-broken' homes and ignore the current parental situation. Secondly, the particular aspects of behaviour investigated differ from one study to another, so that comparison of their results is difficult. Herzog and Sudia (1970), reviewing the findings of a core group of 60 studies concerned to assess the effects of fatherlessness, found that 24 supported the 'classic' view that such homes exerted an adverse influence, 20 challenged this view and 16 reported mixed results. The authors point out, however, that 'the count cannot be taken too seriously because aspects investigated and conclusions reached were so varied and so fragmentary. Most studies of fatherless families look at only one area, and, typically, only a few slivers of information within one area.'

Bearing such reservations in mind, let us look briefly at some of the evidence which other researchers have uncovered.

Personality and social adjustment

The area which has received most attention with regard to the effect of growing up in a one-parent family is that of children's personality and social development. In Britain, the National Survey of Health and Development (Douglas, 1970; Douglas and Blomfield, 1958; Douglas and Ross, 1968) compared children from broken and stable homes in the context of a large-scale, longitudinal study. Using data from this study, Rowntree (1955) found little difference in the incidence of behavioural disturbances such as night terrors, thumb-sucking, nail-biting or eating difficulties when the children in the two types of family situation were aged four years. The only marked variation between the two groups lay in the higher incidence of enuresis among the children from broken homes. Douglas (1970) reported that this difference persisted at each age level studied up to 15 years, and added that 'there is also a general clinical impression that the onset of bedwetting in a previously dry child is often associated with stress within the family.'

In the United States, McCord, McCord and Thurber (1962) investigated the effects of father absence on a group of 55 boys. Their results showed no evidence of a higher incidence of 'abnormal fears' or of 'oral regressive' behaviour (such as thumb-sucking or nail-biting) among these boys than among a control group living with both parents. Russell (1957), using a child guidance clinic sample, compared 174 children from broken homes and a matched sample from intact homes in terms of 11 behavioural characteristics. Although the results showed a tendency for the former group to display more problem behaviour, only in the case of lying and stealing did the differences reach statistical significance. Thomes (1968), comparing the scores of 72 children from broken and intact homes on scales measuring self-concept, attitude to family, and peer relationships, concluded that 'the most meaningful outcome of the study was the finding of many similarities and few differences between children whose fathers had been absent for two or more years and children whose fathers were living in their homes.'

While these and other studies (e.g. Burchinal, 1964; Nye, 1957) draw attention to the similarities between children from broken and intact homes, others claim to show differences in certain areas of behaviour.

A study of illegitimate children (Crellin, Pringle and West, 1971) revealed that, regardless of the family situation in which they were living at the age of seven, those who had stayed with their natural mothers showed a higher incidence of maladjustment than comparable legitimate children, in terms of their scores on the Bristol Social Adjustment Guide. Bartlett and Horrocks (1958) found that adolescents from homes in which one parent had died saw themselves as receiving less recognition and affection from adults and, possibly compensating for this, appeared to seek more attention from the opposite sex. Koch (1961), studying a very small sample of pre-school children from divorced homes found that they showed a higher level of anxiety than a matched group from intact homes.

It seems likely that the apparent contradictions in some of these findings stem from differences in the size and nature of the samples studied and from the fact that the aspects of behaviour investigated varied from one study to another.

Academic attainment

Turning to the field of academic progress and attainment we find that the evidence concerning the effects of a broken family situation is somewhat sparser, and similarly inconclusive. Edwards and Thompson (1971) looked at the scores obtained on a picture intelligence test by approximately 2,500 seven-year-old children in Aberdeen. Comparing the scores of those from fatherless and intact families, they found that, when allowance was made for social class differences, 'there was no evidence that these fatherless children were unduly handicapped in terms of this particular test.' Malmquist (1958), in a study of first-grade Swedish children, found no relationship between reading ability and broken homes.

On the other hand, the National Child Development Study (Pringle, Butler and Davie, 1966) found that, except for children from semi- or unskilled home backgrounds, there were fewer good readers and more poor readers among seven-year-olds living in 'untypical' family situations than among those living with both natural parents. However, the 'untypical' group included a wide variety of parental situations, which might have masked the effects of a particular type of family experience. Using data from the same study, Crellin *et al.* (1971) found that seven-year-old, unadopted illegitimate children did less well in reading and arithmetic than their legitimate counterparts, and that their family situation at the time of the study made little difference to their performance. The National Survey of Health and Development (Douglas and Ross, 1968) showed that, while loss of the father due to sudden death did not seem to affect academic performance, the attainment of children whose fathers had died after a long illness was poorer than expected.

In the United States, Kriesberg (1967) stated that 'there is evidence that fatherless children have lower IQs, are retarded in school and complete fewer years of study than do children in complete families'. Deutsch and Brown (1964) found that children from homes in which the father was absent obtained significantly lower scores on the Lorge-Thorndike Intelligence test, while as far back as 1937 Wallenstein reported that children in families broken by death showed lower IQs and greater retardation in school grade than children from 'normal' home backgrounds.

Although several studies have indicated relatively poor academic attainment among children from broken homes, in many cases it has been suggested that the differences noted between these children and those from intact homes are, for practical purposes, of less significance than the similarities. As Wallenstein pointed out, 'The differences in disfavour of the broken home children are rather small for most of the tests . . . so that broken and normal home children cannot be looked upon psychologically as two distinctly different groups in school'.

Effects on boys and girls

Many writers point out that the loss of one or other parent has different implications for boys and girls. Dager (1964) and Nash (1965) suggest that the importance of the father/son relationship means that boys will be more adversely affected than girls by paternal absence, and a number of previous studies have been concerned only with samples of boys (e.g. Barclay and Cusumano, 1967; Biller 1968, 1969).

The research evidence seems, on the whole, to offer some support for these claims. Wallenstein found greater differences between boys and girls in broken homes than in 'normal' homes in terms of both academic retardation and personality factors, with boys being more adversely affected in each case. Sears' (1951) study of doll play aggression in a sample of very young children found that boys with absent fathers showed less aggressive behaviour than those whose fathers were present, while no differences appeared between comparable groups of girls.

Several other investigators (e.g. Burton and Whiting, 1965; Lynn and Sawrey, 1969) have produced evidence that boys from father-present and father-absent homes differ in respect of certain sex-role oriented aspects of behaviour. Thomes (1968), on the other hand, claims that the 'frequent assumption' that boys would be more affected than girls by father absence was not borne out in his research. In such areas as self-concept and peer-relationships greater differences were found between *girls* whose fathers were present or absent than between similar groups of boys.

Herzog and Sudia (1968) comment that the findings of the numerous studies of sex role development of fatherless children are inconclusive, despite a preponderance of differences showing lower masculinity scores among fatherless boys. They also question the validity of using scores on conventional tests of masculinity/femininity as a criterion of psychological well-being, since not only do such tests fail to cover all aspects of 'masculine' behaviour, but the interpretation and implications to be drawn from the moderate differences found between fatherless and two-parent boys are far from clear.

Age of children in one-parent families

The age of the children under study and also the age at which they lost a parent are further factors of importance in assessing the effects of living in a one-parent family. Most writers claim that the effects are most likely to be adverse when the break in the family occurs during the early period of childhood (Biller, 1969; Hetherington, 1966; Koch, 1961; Nash, 1965; Sears, 1951.) The only differences in delinquency rates found by Douglas (1970) were between boys in unbroken homes and those in families which had been broken in the first six years of the study child's life. Thomes (1968), commenting on the absence of significant differences between children in broken and unbroken homes in his sample, suggested that 'one probably relevant factor is the age of the children studied — 9 to 11 years. If one assumes that this is a period of relative quiescience in personality development for most children, one might expect specific personal and social adjustment problems to be relatively few.'

Cause of the one-parent situation

Finally, the cause of the family breakdown is likely to be of crucial importance for the reactions and subsequent development of the children concerned. Several studies have compared the effects of family disruption due to different causes — usually death or marital break-down. Douglas (1970) showed that divorce and separation *and* the death of the mother were associated with relatively high rates of enuresis up to the age of 15, but that the death of the father was not linked to increased bedwetting at any age.

Rosenberg (1965) found that a relatively high proportion of children from homes broken by divorce or separation showed low self-esteem, while children from families broken by death showed similar scores to those from intact homes. The investigations of Russell (1957) and Wallenstein (1937) both suggested that while children with divorced and separated parents showed more behaviour problems than those from intact families, children from homes broken by death tended to be characterized by academic retardation.

Herzog and Sudia (1968) in their review of research into fatherless families concluded that 'studies that control for type of father absence consistently report differences between children whose fathers are dead and those whose parents are divorced or separated. The differences are not always in the same direction. On the whole, however, ascribed effects of father absence are more marked in children whose parents are divorced or separated than in children whose fathers are dead'. Some writers (Hansen and Hill, 1964; Herzog and Sudia, 1968) suggest that the more marked adverse effects are found in situations where the cause of family breakdown is viewed with social disapproval. Goode (1964) also links the fact that children who have lost a parent through death show lower delinquency rates than children of divorced parents to the social support given to the bereaved, and to the lesser likelihood that the former have 'lived through a period of discussion and quarrelling or problems of identification or loyalty'. This second point highlights a major problem in assessing the effects of marital breakdown on children's development, namely — to what extent is the break in the family itself the crucial factor associated with certain types of behaviour in children, and how far is it merely one possible link in a chain of potentially adverse circumstances? There is some evidence to suggest that the problems of children in unhappy, unbroken families are as great, if not greater, than those found among children living in one-parent families. McCord, McCord and Thurber (1962) point out that 'the evidence ... indicates that many of the effects often presumed to result from paternal absence can largely be attributed to certain parental characteristics — intense conflict, rejection or deviance — which occur more often in broken families'. Rutter (1966) has drawn attention to the relatively high risk of behavioural disturbance among children whose parents suffer from prolonged mental disorder, and West's (1969) study showed that parental pathology was associated with anti-social and delinquent behaviour in children. Nye (1957) suggests that 'the crucial factor in the adjustment of children is the social-psychological success or failure of the family — not whether it is legally or physically broken'.

Summary

From the foregoing pages we have seen that the assessment of the effects of a broken home upon the children concerned is a complex task, and that numerous other relevant factors have to be considered and allowed for. The research evidence so far does not enable us to build up a clear picture of how all the relevant factors interact and influence children's development. The following comments by Herzog and Sudia (1968) give a balanced summing-up of our present state of knowledge:

> 'Existing data do not permit a decisive answer to questions about the effects on children of fatherlessness . . . we would not expect adequate evidence to indicate dramatic differences stemming from father-lessness *per se*. If all the confounding facts could be controlled, children in fatherless homes might be classified as somewhat worse off than children in two-parent homes with regard to some, though by no means all, the variables investigated; but the statistical differences would probably be far less dramatic than is generally assumed and might be negligible'.

The present study thus began amidst a somewhat bewildering array of inconclusive and often contradictory research findings. The value of previous investigations lies less perhaps in the evidence which they have produced than in highlighting the complexities of this area of inquiry. It was with a cautious awareness of these complexities that the design of the present study was undertaken, as will be described in the next two chapters.

Chapter Three

Background to the study

We have already seen in Chapter Two that previous investigations into the one-parent family and its effects upon children have been somewhat fragmentary, and their results often conflicting and inconclusive. One reason for this no doubt lies in the sheer difficulty of carrying out such a study. Firstly, there is the problem of obtaining a large, representative sample of one-parent children, together with an equally representative group of children from 'normal' two-parent homes with whom they can be compared. Secondly, only by collecting a great deal of information about families and their environment, and about various aspects of the children's development, can a complete picture be built up of the characteristics of different types of family situation and the ways in which these influence their children.

A third, perhaps less essential but nonetheless important element in such an investigation is the need to study the progress and development of the children concerned over a period of time. A particular family situation is not a static set of circumstances but a dynamic ongoing process. Thus, the period of stress which may precede the loss of a parent, together with subsequent changes in the family's circumstances and in the relationships between its remaining members, may have effects upon children's development which can only be traced over a period of time.

All three of the conditions mentioned above were met by the National Child Development Study, a longitudinal follow-up of a large, representative sample of children selected only by their date of birth. This study grew out of the earlier Perinatal Mortality Survey (1958) of the same group of children, and provided an unprecedented opportunity to study those who were found to have experienced life in a one-parent family, and to compare their development with that of the rest of the cohort.

The Perinatal Mortality Survey and the follow-up studies which have been completed to date are described briefly below. For the reader who would like to know more about any aspects of this research, references are given to the major publications which have arisen from the studies.

The Perinatal Mortality Survey

This investigation, which was sponsored by the National Birthday Trust Fund, was set up in 1958 to study the administration of maternity services in Great Britain and the causes of perinatal death (still-births and deaths in the first week of life) (Butler and Alberman, 1969; Butler and Bonham, 1963). In order to do this, information was collected on almost every baby born in England, Scotland and Wales during the week 3rd—9th March in that year. The resulting cohort, numbering some 17,000 births, contained an estimated 98 per cent of all babies born in that week, and as such constituted a uniquely representative national sample. In addition, the comprehensive nature of the medical, social and obstetric information obtained was un-paralleled anywhere for such a national cohort.

The National Child Development Study

The aim of the National Child Development Study, set up in 1964 by the National Children's Bureau, was to trace the subsequent progress and development of the children who had been the subjects of the Perinatal Mortality Survey. So far, two follow-up investigations have been completed, the first in 1965 when the children were seven years old, and the second in 1969 when they were aged eleven.

At each follow-up stage, a wealth of information was collected from several different sources about various aspects of the children's background and development. Firstly, a structured interview was carried out by a health visitor, usually with the child's mother, or in some cases with the father or other caring adult. This provided details about the home environment, such as the composition of the family, the parents' occupational and educational background, the type of accommodation occupied and so on, plus information concerning the child's development and current behaviour.

An educational assessment form, completed by the head teachers and class teachers of the schools attended by the sample children, provided information about the school and its organization, contacts between school and home, and an assessment of each child's ability, attainment and adjustment in school. In addition, the children themselves completed a series of ability and attainment tests.

Finally, each child in the study underwent a comprehensive medical examination, which included measurements of height and weight, tests of vision, speech and hearing and a full clinical examination. The information relating to each child was recorded on a coded form by the examining school medical officer.

The results of the study of the seven-year-old children have already been published (Davie, Butler and Goldstein, 1972; Pringle, Butler and Davie, 1966). Analysis of the material collected when the children were eleven is nearing completion, while a third follow-up is currently being carried out. This survey is of particular interest since the children concerned, now aged sixteen, belong to the first year group to experience an extra year of compulsory education following the raising of the school-leaving age.

It is further hoped that this unique picture of growth and development can be completed by following the cohort right through to adulthood, perhaps even until the children themselves become parents. The study is already unrivalled in the comprehensive view which it provides of the health, environment, attainment and behaviour of a large representative sample of children at different stages in their development. Moreover, the size of the sample has made it possible to carry out separate studies of special groups of children, for example, those suffering from particular handicaps, those who were born illegitimate (Crellin, Pringle and West, 1971), adopted children (Seglow, Pringle and Wedge, 1972), socially disadvantaged children (Wedge and Prosser, 1973) children identified as 'gifted' (Hitchfield, 1974), those who come into care (Mapstone, 1969), and as we are concerned with in this report, children living in one-parent families.

Perhaps the greatest value of the study, however, lies in its longitudinal aspect. One of the inherent difficulties of social research lies in the fact that people cannot be experimentally subjected to the kinds of conditions which are of interest to investigators. A *post facto* identification of one-parent families, however, would mean that only current information would be available and that crucial data relating to earlier stages in the family situation would be at best retrospective and unreliable. Also, if the only data available were of a cross-sectional nature, it would not be possible to study changes in the family's structure and environment which may follow the loss of a parent. A longitudinal study on the other hand enables us to discover not only how many children lose a parent, but how long their families remain in this situation and in what ways they adapt to it. In addition, such information makes it possible to look at the *long-term* effects of the loss of a parent upon the various aspects of the children's environment and development with which we are concerned.

Chapter Four

Aims and design of the research

The investigation was set up in 1970 at the request of the Department of Health and Social Security, so that preliminary findings could be submitted as evidence in the Finer Committee on one-parent families (1974)[1]

Aims of the study

The broad aims of the study can be summarized under three main headings:

1) *Prevalence of one-parent family situations* How many children in the National Child Development Study sample had experienced life in a one-parent family? How had these situations come about and how long did they continue?

2) *Background and environment of children in one-parent families* How did children in one and two-parent families compare in terms of such factors as social class background, size of family and age of parents? Did their material circumstances differ, for example, with regard to financial resources and the type and quality of accommodation occupied? To what extent did the employment situation of mothers and fathers who were lone parents resemble that of their counterparts in 'intact' families?

---

1 The limited time available for the first part of the project restricted the type of analysis which could be undertaken. The interim report, which was submitted to the Finer Committee in August 1971, contained preliminary information on the prevalence of one-parent families in the National Child Development Study at each follow-up stage, plus a description of certain characteristics of children in these and two-parent families, such as social class background, family size, type of accommodation, income and employment.

3) *Effects of family situation on children's development* Taking account of any differences in the home background and environment of children in one and two-parent families, in what ways was their family situation related to their development in terms of educational progress and attainment, social and psychological adjustment, aspirations for the future and physical health?

The Sample

What is a one-parent family? What do we mean when we refer to a child as being 'fatherless' or 'motherless'? It was pointed out in Chapter Two that other studies have varied widely in the definitions employed; for instance, children with a step-parent are sometimes included in the 'broken home' category and in other cases are regarded as living in 'intact' homes.

The problem of defining a one-parent family appears to have no clear-cut solution, and any definition must be to some extent arbitrary. The essence of the problem lies, perhaps, in the question of what it means to be a parent. To consider only the physical presence or absence of one or other natural parent is to ignore this crucial question of what constitutes the parental role. Marsden (1969) defines a fatherless family as one which 'lacks a person who embodies the expectations, duties and functions usually fulfilled by a father'. Thus, even when the natural fàther is absent, another male relative or friend may provide financial and emotional support for the mother and children, so that in such respects at least the family does not lack a father figure. Conversely, a natural father may be present in the family household and yet perform so inadequately in the various aspects of the paternal role that, in functional terms, his children experience many of the deprivations of fatherlessness.

The definition employed in the present investigation was determined to a large extent by the nature of the data available from the National Child Development Study. At each follow-up survey, information was obtained as to whether the study child was normally cared for by his or her natural mother and father or by one or more parent substitutes. A large-scale survey such as this could not hope to provide details of family situations and relationships which would permit an evaluation of the quality of 'parenting' provided by a natural father or mother, or of how far a 'substitute' was fulfilling the role of a natural parent. However, it would seem reasonable to suppose that a child living with, say, his mother and step-father, or one cared for by her father and grandmother, would be experiencing a very different home environment from a child looked after singlehanded by just one natural parent.

Consequently, for the purposes of the present study, a child was regarded as living in a one-parent family if, at the time of survey, he or she was *being cared for by a natural mother or father alone, without help from a parent substitute of the opposite sex living in the same household*.

Excluded from the one-parent sample were a small number of children being cared for by one parent *substitute* alone. It was felt that these children might constitute a particularly 'anomalous' group, possibly differing in certain important respects from those living with one natural parent alone.

Control sample

Throughout the study comparisons were made between children living in one-parent families as defined above and those living in in 'normal' two-parent homes. This control group contained all children being cared for by both their natural parents at the time of the follow-up survey. Although it was suggested above that step-parents or other parent substitutes may in some respects re-constitute a family unit, such situations could clearly not be equated with those which, as far as could be ascertained, had never experienced any rupture or structural change.

Sub-groups of children in one-parent families

In each area of analysis comparisons were made not only between one and two-parent children, but also *within* the fatherless and motherless groups, according to whether the situation was the result of the death of a parent, marital breakdown or illegitimacy. It would seem likely that the factors producing a one-parent home would be of major importance in determining its effects upon the members of the family concerned and upon their subsequent circumstances and adaptation to the situation. It might be hypothesized that, except in cases involving the stresses of long-term illness, a child who loses a parent through death will, in general, have experienced a secure, stable home environment prior to the bereavement whereas a boy or girl whose home is broken by marital discord is likely to have suffered from a period of tension and bitterness in the home before the final break occurred which produced a one-parent family. Again, an illegitimate child of an unmarried mother will not have experienced the *loss* of a parent in the same sense as the child whose home is broken. Thus, although the immediate 'cause' of the one-parent situation may represent a somewhat crude classification which inevitably ignores wide variations in individual cases, it was felt essential to maintain these separate categories when analysing the findings from the study.

Method of analysis

In many of the areas of inquiry, both cross-sectional and longitudinal analyses were carried out; the first in order to compare children in one and two-parent families at a particular point in time, the second to examine the relative *change* shown by the different groups over a period. Most of the cross-sectional analyses used material collected for the second follow-up study when the children were aged eleven. For these analyses the one-parent group included *all* children living in a motherless or fatherless family at that time. The longitudinal analyses, on the other hand, were concerned to measure *change* in circumstances, behaviour and performance between the first and second follow-up surveys, and for this purpose the children's parental situation at both seven and eleven years had to be taken into consideration. As a result, the following sub-groups formed the sample for the longitudinal analyses:

1) Children in fatherless families at both seven and eleven
2) Children in two-parent families at seven, fatherless families at eleven
3) Children in two-parent families at seven, motherless families at eleven
4) Children in two-parent families at both seven and eleven.

Owing to the small number of children concerned (18) it was unfortunately not possible to study as a separate group those who had been living in a motherless family at both seven and eleven years of age.

Presentation of the results

Wherever reference is made in the text to differences between groups of children, these have been tested and found to be statistically significant, unless otherwise stated. An account of the statistical techniques employed in the research is given in Appendix 1.

Throughout the book the results of comparisons between different groups are presented quantitatively, usually in the form of percentages. In order to minimize the cost of producing the report however, the bulk of the tables summarizing the findings have not been included.[1] Throughout the text, references to tables which are contained in Appendix 2 of this report are pre-fixed with the letter A. Those which are lodged with the British Library have the prefix S.

---

1 For the reader who is interested in studying these, copies are obtainable at cost price from: The Supplementary Publications Scheme, British Library (Lending Division) Boston Spa, Yorkshire LS23 7BO, quoting reference no. SUP81002.

'Children' and 'families'

It will be clear from the foregoing description of the National Child Development Study that the sample involved is one of *children* and not one of *families*. For ease of reporting however, reference is sometimes made in the text to 'families', 'mothers' or 'fathers'. In studying working mothers for example, it is less cumbersome to refer to the number of widows who had jobs than to the level of maternal employment among children who had been bereaved. It should be remembered however, that in each area of inquiry, the unit of analysis is the *child*.

Follow-up study of one-parent families

As mentioned earlier the data collected for the National Child Development Study provided an unprecedented opportunity to compare the background and development of a representative sample of children from one and two-parent families. However, since the follow-up surveys were designed to monitor the development of a large, nationally representative sample of children, it was not possible to include questions which would have been of particular interest in relation to specific groups, such as children living in one parent homes.

It was felt important, however, to find out more about these children and their families, and so a special follow-up study was mounted in the autumn of 1972, supported by a grant from the Buttle Trust.

The aim of this project, which included a sample of all the children living in one-parent families at eleven, was to collect information about the problems posed by the absence of a parent, the ways in which these had been dealt with, including the amount of help received from various sources and the perceived effects of the situation upon the remaining parent and children. The method of investigation employed was an intensive interview carried out with the parents concerned, and the findings of this inquiry are published as a companion volume to the present report (Ferri and Robinson, 1976).

Chapter Five

The size of the problem

In 1971, according to the Finer Report (1974), more than a million children in Britain were living in homes with only one parent. At the same time, one-parent families formed about one-tenth of all families with children. That so little is known about the effects of such situations is thus a serious gap in our knowledge about a large, and probably growing, minority of children.

What such figures do not tell us however, is how many children lose one or both parents. At any given time there will be a great many children living in a variety of 'anomalous' care situations as a result of family disorganization of some kind, and those being brought up by one natural parent alone will represent only a proportion of these. It was decided, therefore to begin the present investigation by looking at the total number of children who, at each follow-up stage of the National Child Development Study, were no longer being cared for by both their natural parents.

How many children lose a parent?

By the time the children in the study were aged seven, eight per cent of the total sample were no longer living with both parents. Four years later, when they were eleven-years-old, the number had risen to over eleven per cent (table 5.1). This latter figure is identical to that quoted by Edwards and Thompson (1971) in their study of 2,511 nine- to fourteen-year-old children in Aberdeen. Douglas (1970) too, found that, at the age of fifteen, eleven per cent of the children in the National Survey of Health and Development were no longer in the care of both natural parents. While one might expect a higher figure among a group of older children, the exclusion of illegitimate children from Douglas' sample would have reduced the proportion living in 'anomalous' parental situations.

The Plowden report (1967) contains details of a national survey carried out in 1964, which found that, in a sample of over 3,000 parents of seven, eight and eleven-year-old children, at least eight per cent of homes were lacking one or both natural parents.

Table 5.1: Parental care situation of children in National Child Development Study sample when they were seven and when they were eleven.

Parental care situation	children aged 7		children aged 11	
	N	%	N	%
Living with both natural parents	13,514	92.0	12,285	88.6
not living with both natural parents	1,174	8.0	1,581	11.4
total for whom information available	14,688	100.0	13,866	100.0

Table 5.2 shows the number of children at seven and at eleven who had lost their father, their mother or both parents. It should be pointed out that the latter group contains a large proportion of children (198 at age seven and 130 at age eleven) who had been adopted at or soon after birth, so that they had not 'lost' both natural parents in the same sense as the other children.

Table 5.2: Number of children in National Child Development Study sample who had lost father, mother or both natural parents.

	children aged 7		children aged 11	
	N	% of total sample	N	% of total sample
lost father only	737	5.0	1,067	7.7
lost mother only	111	0.8	237	1.7
lost both parents[1]	326	2.2	277	2.0
Total	1,174	8.0	1,581	11.4

At each age level, the fatherless considerably outnumber the motherless, although the ratio drops from six and a half to one at seven years to four and a half to one at the age of eleven. Thus, while the total number of children who had lost their father increased by less than a half during the four year period, the number who had lost their mother more than doubled. Our data did not permit closer investigation of this difference but a partial explanation may be that, in cases of marital

1   This drop between seven and eleven in the number who had lost both parents is largely due to the fact that information was missing at eleven on a number of children living with adoptive parents at seven.

breakdown, the proportion of children remaining with their father increased with a rise in the age of the children concerned. Looking at the findings of other studies in this area, it would certainly appear that the ratio of fatherless to motherless is related to the age of the children in the sample. Rowntree (1955) found that fatherless outnumbered motherless by seven to one among four year-old children in the National Survey of Health and Development while Douglas (1970) found a ratio of only three and a half to one when the same children were aged fifteen.

Parental care situation following the loss of a parent

What happened to the large number of children who had lost one or both parents by the time they were seven or eleven? An examination of the family circumstances of these children at the time of each follow-up survey revealed more than 30 different types of 'anomalous' parental situation. It would clearly have been impossible to treat each group separately, especially since many cases involved only one or two children. Also, since our main concern was with those who had lost one parent and remained in the care of the other, it was decided to confine our further analysis to these children.

It was clear from the information concerning the care situation at the time of the surveys that, at both seven and eleven, a considerable proportion of the children who had lost a mother or father were not actually living in a one-parent family; the remaining parent having either remarried or obtained the assistance of a parent 'substitute' of the opposite sex living in the same household (tables A5.3 and A5.4). It should be emphasized that no attempt could be made to evaluate the extent to which any 'substitute' parent was fulfilling the role of the missing father or mother. The figures referred to are based on information obtained at each follow-up survey concerning the male and female adults who were 'acting as the child's parents'.

In the case of motherless children the most common mother 'substitutes' were a grandmother or elder sister, while among those who had lost their father, a grandfather was by far the most frequently mentioned 'father figure'.

The data also revealed marked differences in the subsequent family situations of children who had lost their father and those whose mother was missing. At each age level the proportions whose remaining parent had remarried (or in a few cases, were cohabiting) were very similar, (about one in three in each case), but a much higher proportion of fathers had the assistance of another parent substitute. It would appear then .that mothers were much more likely than fathers to be caring for their children single-handed following the loss of their partner. These findings may well reflect differences in our society's attitudes towards men and women as sole parents; as Sanctuary and Whitehead (1970) put it: 'The figure of the deserted male left to look after children is one that attracts sympathetic assistance from every quarter. Why is it that the deserted woman in exactly the same position is less appealing to our society?' Not only sympathy perhaps, but society's expectation that a father left on his own will continue to go out to work is reflected in Marsden's (1969) comment 'that a father without a wife can usually call on female kin to bring up his children, or he can advertise with community approval for a housekeeper'. Such initiatives, however, are not open to the husbandless mother seeking a father substitute for her children as our present findings would seem to reflect.

Cause of family breakdown in one-parent families

Next an examination was made of the cause of the family breakdown which had resulted in the children subsequently being cared for by their remaining parent alone.[1]

When the children in the study were aged eleven, 652 (4.7 per cent of the total sample) were being cared for by their mother alone, and 98 (0.7 per cent) were living with their father in homes without a mother figure. Information was obtained during the parental interviews concerning the circumstances which had led to these situations. Among the fatherless children just over half of the cases were the result of marital breakdown, 35 per cent were due to the father's death and nine per cent of the children were illegitimate (Table A5.5). The 'marital breakdown' category includes cases of divorce, separation and desertion, since it was unfortunately not possible from the survey data to distinguish these situations. It is clear that these three categories may represent very different situations not only with regard to the material and environmental circumstances of the families concerned but also in terms of the emotional effects upon both parents and children. However, there are likely to be as wide variations *within* each group as between them in respect of such factors, which a survey-type investigation could not hope to assess. Also, since we will be concerned with the long-term development of the children in the sample, it would be particularly difficult to allow for changes in circumstances which may have arisen between surveys e.g. cases in which separation or desertion had proceeded to divorce.

It was interesting to find that only a small minority, namely, one in eleven of the fatherless children, and one in thirteen of all those living

---

1 While it would have been more meaningful perhaps to look at the cause of breakdown among *all* children who had lost a parent, this was not possible, since such information was not available for a substantial proportion of children living with step-parents.

in one-parent families at eleven, were illegitimate children being cared for by an unsupported mother. This finding clearly challenges the popular belief that the 'typical' one-parent family consists of an unmarried mother bringing up an illegitimate child.

As far as the motherless children were concerned, approximately half of the cases were due to marital breakdown and half to the death of the child's mother.

It would seem likely that the age of the children in the sample concerned bears some relation to the proportion of cases due to various causes. There was some evidence from the present study that families in which the father had died represented an increasing proportion of all fatherless families as the sample children grew older. The number of cases of fatherlessness due to death increased by nearly three-quarters in the four years between the two surveys, while those resulting from marital breakdown rose by only fifty per cent (Table S5.6). Douglas, (1970) also found that among the children in the National Survey of Health and Development, divorce and separation as a cause of family breakdown tended to be concentrated in the early years.

Boys and girls in one-parent families

The numbers of boys and girls in families which were fatherless or motherless due to a parent's death were roughly similar (Table S5.7). Also, there were almost equal numbers of each sex who were fatherless as a result of illegitimacy. However, an interesting difference was found in the number of boys and girls living in fatherless and motherless families as a result of marital breakdown. In cases where the father was absent 55 per cent of the children concerned were girls and only 45 per cent boys, while among the motherless children boys outnumbered girls (63 per cent compared with 37 per cent). Thus, although the majority of both boys and girls remained with their mother following the breakdown of a marriage, (88 per cent altogether), there also appeared to be a tendency for children to be cared for by the parent of the same sex.

How long do children remain in one-parent families?

It was unfortunately not possible to tell from the information available just how long all the children who lost a parent remained in a one-parent family situation. However, an examination of the family circumstances at eleven years of those children who were being cared for by their mothers alone at the age of seven provided some insight into the dynamics of the situation. Such information was available for 359[1] of the 418 children concerned. This showed that three-quarters of

---

1 Lack of information for 59 of the 418 children reflects a higher rate of attrition among the fatherless than among the rest of the cohort at the second follow-up stage. It is thus likely that the number of children found to be in one-parent families at eleven is an underestimate.

the children were still being cared for by their mother alone when they were eleven (Table S5.8). Only one mother in five had remarried (or was cohabiting) and provided the child with a stepfather. The highest rate of remarriage (25 per cent) was found among mothers who had experienced marital breakdown, although, since this group included separated and deserted wives, the figure for divorced mothers would clearly be considerably higher. Only 15 per cent of widowed mothers had married and nine per cent of those with illegitimate children.[1]

These findings should be interpreted with caution, as no account could be taken of the total length of time which had elapsed since the loss of the child's father, and this may have varied between the different groups. However, the differences found between divorced and widowed mothers correspond to those quoted by other investigators both in this country and in the United States. (Fletcher, 1962; Goode, 1965; Kriesberg, 1970; Marsden, 1969; Rowntree, 1955).

The number of children being cared for by their father alone at seven (33) was too small to permit a similar analysis of their care situation at eleven. However, an examination of the family circumstances of *all* children living with their own father but not their own mother at eleven, showed no relationship between the cause of family breakdown and the care situation which had followed it (Table S5.9). Thus, unlike mothers left on their own, fathers who had been bereaved were no less likely to have remarried than were those who had experienced marital breakdown.

Summary

At the age of seven, eight per cent of the children in the National Child Development Study sample were no longer being cared for by both natural parents; by the time they were eleven the figure was eleven per cent. Fatherless children outnumbered those who had lost their mother by approximately six and a half to one at the age of seven, and four and a half to one at eleven years.

At both seven and eleven, children who had lost their father were more likely to be living in a one-parent family than those who had lost their mother, as the latter group contained a higher proportion who were subsequently cared for by a parent substitute. Among the eleven year-old children, marital breakdown was responsible for just over half of the cases of fatherlessness, the death of the father for thirty-five per cent and illegitimacy for a further nine per cent. Among the children

---

1 This figure does not of course, give an accurate indication of the marriage rate among mothers of all illegitimate children, since it is likely that the rate would be higher at or soon after the child's birth, and these children would not have been included in the present sample.

who had lost their mother, half of the cases were due to marital breakdown and half to the mother's death.

Three-quarters of the children cared for by their mothers alone at seven were still in that situation four years later. Mothers who had been divorced showed a higher rate of remarriage than those who had been widowed.

Chapter Six

Background characteristics of children in one-parent families

In this chapter we look at some of the general social and demographic characteristics of our sample of one-parent children, including their social class background, the number of children in the family, and the age of their remaining parent.

Social Class

The National Child Development Study, in common with most other investigations, took the occupation of the male head of the household as an indicator of social class. The classification used was that adopted by the Registrar General for the national census (HMSO, 1960). An immediate problem thus arose in the present study in assessing the social class background of children in fatherless families, since no current occupational information was available for these families at the time of the follow-up surveys. To overcome this difficulty, it was decided to use father's occupation at the time of the child's *birth* as an index of social class background for the majority of children in one and two-parent families. Although more recent information was available for those in two-parent and motherless families, it was considered essential to employ the same definition for all groups, so that valid comparisons could be made between them.

Only the illegitimate children whose mothers were unsupported at the time of their birth were lacking information concerning father's occupation. For this group it was decided to take mother's *father's* job at the time of the child's birth as being the best available indicator of social class background. It should be borne in mind, however, that this information is not strictly comparable to that referring to children in other family situations.

Family situation and social class

First of all a comparison was made of the social class background of children cared for by both their natural parents at the age of eleven and that of children living in some kind of 'anomalous' family situation. This showed a marked difference between the two groups, with the latter containing fewer children of professional and managerial workers and a higher proportion whose fathers had had unskilled jobs (Table S6.1). The proportion of children *not* living with both parents was lowest in social classes 1 and 2 (only one child in eighteen), and highest by far in social class 5 (almost one child in every seven).

These findings contrast with those of the National Survey quoted in the Plowden Report (1967) which, looking at father's occupation when last living in the household, found no significant association between the proportion of broken homes and social class. The National Survey of Health and Development (Douglas, 1970; Rowntree, 1955) likewise found little relationship between social class background and the proportion of broken and intact homes (although this sample excluded all illegitimate children). Comparing the social class background of all children living in fatherless homes at eleven with that of children in two-parent families also showed a marked difference, with the fatherless group containing a larger number whose fathers had been employed in semi- or unskilled jobs (30 per cent compared with 21 per cent (Table A6.2)). However, there were also differences *among* the fatherless children according to the reason for their family situation. Those whose fathers had died did not in fact differ significantly from those living with both parents as far as social class background was concerned. It was where marital breakdown had occurred that the disproportionate numbers from semi- or unskilled backgrounds were concentrated (32 per cent compared with 25 per cent of widows' children and 21 per cent of those from two-parent homes).

Altogether 43 per cent of the illegitimate children had mothers who themselves had come from a semi- or unskilled home as measured by their fathers' occupation. As pointed out earlier, however, caution should be exercised in comparing these children with the other groups in view of the different measure of social class adopted.

Children living in motherless homes at the age of eleven were also more likely to have fathers employed in semi- or unskilled occupations (27 per cent) than those cared for by both parents (21 per cent). Unlike the fatherless families, however, there were no social class differences between families in which the mother had died and those in which marital breakdown had occurred, although the numbers involved were rather small.

George and Wilding (1972) in their study of motherless families also found that relatively few of the lone fathers had professional and

managerial occupations, although they attributed this in part to the
selective nature of their sample, a shortcoming which does not apply to
the present study.

The importance of social class background defined in terms of
occupational level lies in its usefulness as an indirect measure of broader
features of a family's material environment and way of life, which in
turn are related to various aspects of children's development. Thus, in
making further comparisons between children in one and two-parent
families it was clearly necessary to make some allowance for the social
class differences which have been reported here. In all subsequent
analyses, therefore, children from non-manual and manual backgrounds
have been studied separately.[1] In view of the very small number of
motherless children whose fathers had non-manual occupations (17),
analyses for this group which took account of social class were confined
to those from manual homes. Illegitimate children were excluded from
all such analyses, since the different measure of social class available for
these children made such comparisons of questionable validity.

Family size

The definition of family size employed in the National Child
Development Study was the number of children under 21 years of age
currently living in the study child's household. Any definition will, of
course, be somewhat arbitrary, and it should be pointed out that this
particular criterion would include a number of non-dependent children,
as well as a small proportion who were not, in fact, siblings of the child
in the study.

Using the above definition, little overall difference was found in the
family size distribution of fatherless and two-parent families (Table
A6.3(a)). Not unexpectedly however, the number of only children in
the illegitimate group (41 per cent) was four times greater than among
children living with both parents (10 per cent). There was also a
relatively high proportion of only children in families where the father
had died (18 per cent). In neither case however, did the overall
distribution differ significantly from that in the two-parent group.
Among children who were fatherless due to marital breakdown, the
family size distribution closely resembled that of children in complete
families.

A similar pattern emerged when social class background was taken
into account, although among children from manual homes, the
difference in family size between those whose fathers had died and
those whose mothers were divorced or separated did reach statistical

---

1   The non-manual group included social classes 1, 2 and 3 non-manual, and the
manual group social classes 3 manual, 4 and 5.

significance. The former group contained a higher proportion of only children than the latter (19 per cent as against 11 per cent) and fewer large families of four or more children (27 per cent and 38 per cent respectively) (Table S6.3 (c)).

The only other large-scale study to compare family size in broken and intact families was that of Rowntree (1955), whose findings contrasted with those reported here, in showing that bereaved families tended to be larger, and divorced or separated families smaller, than families headed by both parents. It is likely, however, that these discrepancies could be accounted for by differences in the ages of the children in the two samples, and by possible peculiarities in the pattern of family disorganization in Rowntree's immediately post-war sample.

It is difficult to interpret the reported differences in family size between our two fatherless groups without additional information, such as the duration of the marriages within each group. It will be seen later in this chapter however, that the widows in the sample were, on average, considerably older than the divorced and separated mothers. It is likely therefore that the widows' families contained more children who were over 21 or living away from home, and who would thus have been excluded from the present definition of family size.

Whatever the reason for the apparent difference between the two groups it does seem likely that the number of dependent children left in her care will have implications for the nature and degree of the problems facing an unsupported mother. In view of this, the relatively high proportion of large families among the mothers whose marriage had broken down were borne in mind when factors such as housing, employment and income were investigated.

A comparison of the number of children in motherless and two-parent families revealed a marked difference between the two groups, both overall and when social class background was taken into account. Almost a quarter (24 per cent) of the motherless sample were only children, compared with just one in ten of those living with both parents (Table A6.3 (a)). At the other end of the scale, the number of large families (four or more children) in the two groups were 22 per cent and 31 per cent respectively. In contrast with the findings on fatherless families, the cause of the mother's absence did not appear to be in any way related to family size.

Widowers tended to be older than fathers in two-parent families and it may be that, as was suggested in the case of widows, their families contained a disproportionate number of older children who would not have been included in our definition of family size. In families which were motherless due to divorce or separation, it seems possible (as the findings in the next section indicate) that some of the children of the family were cared for by the mother following the breakdown of the parents' marriage. These two factors together could well account for the overall smaller family size found among the motherless children, when compared with those in two-parent homes.

Number of children with siblings living away from home

Information was also available concerning the number of children of the family who were under 21 years of age and who were *not* living in the study child's household at the time of the follow-up survey. This included, for example, married siblings, those in residential homes or schools who were home only for holidays, members of the armed forces and children being brought up by relatives or, in some cases, estranged parents.

A comparison between children in different family situations showed that 15 per cent of those in fatherless families had one or more siblings not living at home, as against only six per cent of children in two-parent families (Table S6.4). There was little difference among the fatherless children according to the reason for their father's absence.

As many as one in five of the motherless children had brothers or sisters who were living away from home, and the highest proportion of all (27 per cent) was found among those who were motherless as a result of marital breakdown. Although the numbers involved were small, and it was not possible to look at the reasons for absence from home in each case, it seems possible that where divorce or separation had occurred, it was not unusual for the children of the family to be split between father and mother. This was already suggested in Chapter Five, which showed a slight tendency for children to be found in the care of the same-sex parent following a breakdown in marriage.

Whatever the reason for the one-parent situation the present findings suggest that not only have such families been disrupted by the loss of a parent, but that they may have been further fragmented by the absence of one or more children as a direct or indirect result of this breakdown.

Age of parents

The age of parents left to bring up children on their own may have implications for the ways in which they react and adapt to the situation. Younger parents are likely to be better able to cope with the sheer physical strain of total responsibility, their chances of re-marriage will be greater and their employment prospects more favourable. Older mothers, in particular, may find great difficulty in resuming work after many years at home or in taking up employment perhaps for the very first time. In their study of motherless families, George and Wilding (1972) showed that fathers left on their own may be forced to change their jobs in order to cope with their altered circumstances. Such a course of action may prove difficult, if not impossible, for middle-aged men in an economic context of high unemployment and earlier redundancy or retirement.

For the purposes of this study, the age of the parent concerned was that given at the time of the eleven-year-old follow-up, and not when the family breakdown occurred. Thus, the ages referred to here will be rather higher than at the time the family lost a parent. A further complicating factor is that age at marriage could not be taken into account, although in view of the relationship between social class background and age at marriage, it was hoped to allow for this to some extent by analysing the data for non-manual and manual groups separately.

Other studies of the age of mothers in one-parent families have shown that widows tend to be older than mothers who are divorced or separated or who have illegitimate children (Marsden, 1969; Rowntree, 1955). Such findings are hardly surprising, since bereavement is more likely to occur at a later stage in life than marital breakdown or the birth of an illegitimate child.

The results from the present study confirm these trends. Comparing firstly the mothers living in two-parent families with those whose husbands had died, showed a highly significant difference in age distribution, both overall and at each social class level, with the widowed mothers tending to be older. Altogether more than two-thirds of the widows were aged 40 or over when the study child was eleven, compared with only four out of ten mothers in unbroken families (Table S6.5 (a)).

The opposite trend appeared when mothers in two-parent families were compared with those who had experienced marital breakdown. Here there were more *younger* mothers among the latter group — seven out of ten were under forty at the time of the survey. Again, this difference remained when social class background was taken into account (Tables S6.5 (b) and (c)).

The age difference between widows and mothers whose marriage had broken down was thus even more marked, with over two-thirds of the latter group aged under 40 at the time of survey compared with less than one-third of all the widows.

Contrary to other research findings, (Marsden, 1969; Wimperis, 1960) there was little difference in the age distribution of mothers with illegitimate children and those in two-parent families. The present illegitimate sample is small, however, and it should be emphasized that it is a highly selective group (i.e. mothers caring alone for eleven-year-old illegitimate children). It is clearly not representative of *all* mothers having illegitimate children who, as the Registrar General's figures show, tend to be younger than those giving birth to legitimate babies. In fact, almost half (46 per cent) of the mothers of illegitimate

children in the present sample were aged 40 or more at the time of the
survey, so that most of these would have been 30 or over when the
study child was born. These findings would seem to suggest that the age
of a mother at the birth of an illegitimate child is related to the
likelihood that she will be left to bring up the child singlehanded.

Looking at the ages of the fathers of the eleven-year-old children
showed that, as was the case with widows, fathers who had been
bereaved were older than fathers in two-parent homes. Eighty-two per
cent of widowers were aged 40 or over at the time of the survey,
compared with only 58 per cent of fathers in unbroken families. (Table
S6.6 (a)).

However, while mothers whose marriage had broken down tended to
be younger than mothers in two-parent families, there was no such
difference in the age distribution of divorced and separated fathers and
those living in unbroken homes. A similar pattern emerged when a
separate analysis was made of the age distribution of fathers in manual
occupations (Table S6.6 (b)).

The only other study which has looked at the ages of fathers looking
after children on their own is that of George and Wilding (1972), who
also found that widowers tended on average to be considerably older
than fathers who had been divorced or separated.

Summary

A study of the social class background of the children in our sample
revealed little difference between those in two-parent families and those
whose fathers had died. Children living with divorced and separated
mothers, however, were more likely to have had fathers in semi- or
unskilled occupations. A relatively high proportion of semi- and
unskilled workers was also found among the lone fathers, regardless of
the reason for their family situation.

There was little overall difference in family size between fatherless
and two-parent children, although widows' families tended to be rather
smaller than those of divorced and separated mothers, particularly at
the manual level. The illegitimate group contained the highest proportion of only children. Motherless families were smaller than those
with both parents present, regardless of the cause of breakdown. All
one-parent families were more likely than those with both parents
present to have children living away from home, and the proportion
was particularly high among families which were motherless as a result
of marital breakdown.

Widows and widowers were, on average, considerably older than
their counterparts in complete families. Divorced and separated
mothers on the other hand were younger than mothers in two-parent
families, but there was no difference in the age distribution of fathers
whose marriage had broken down and those in unbroken homes.

Chapter Seven

The financial position of children in one-parent families

Chapter One looked at the role and function of the modern family in providing for the economic, social and emotional needs of its members. Our present day society is organized in such a way that the achievement of an adequate standard of living for a family normally requires one parent, usually the father, to undertake full-time employment outside the home, while the developmental needs of young children are optimally met by the more or less constant presence and attention of a caring adult, conventionally the mother. At first sight then, the loss of the father would appear to entail primarily an economic threat and the mother's absence to present first and foremost a problem of child care. However, in practical terms the two are indissolubly linked, and the difficulty facing any lone parent is one of combining these apparently incompatible full-time roles of breadwinner and homemaker without an unacceptable reduction of standards in one area or in both.

In this chapter we look at the impact of the loss or absence of one parent upon the material living standards of the families concerned, in terms of their basic economic resources.

Poverty in one-parent families

During the past decade or so there has been an accumulation of evidence to suggest that one-parent, particularly fatherless, families suffer from financial hardship, if not actual poverty, and that the loss or absence of a parent seriously jeopardises a family's standard of living. Actual estimates of the degree of poverty in any population will, of course, differ according to the samples studied and the criterion of poverty adopted, both of which are subject to considerable variation. However, the available evidence leaves little room for doubt that fatherless families are economically at a disadvantage when compared with those in which both parents are present. A Government report (*Circumstances of Families*, 1967) estimated that about 50 per cent of fatherless families with two or more children had 'initial resources less than their requirements' as assessed by reference to Supplementary Benefit rates. A study carried out by the Government Social Survey and published in the Plowden Report (1967) took actual income level as a measure, and found that while only one 'normal' family in a hundred had a weekly income of £10 or less, the figure for fatherless families was 35 per cent. More recently, the Finer Committee (1974) concluded that the evidence available to them 'overwhelmingly confirmed the general impression of financial hardship amongst one-parent families.'

One-parent families and state support

As suggested above, poverty is a notoriously difficult concept to define and the measures employed will vary from time to time and from place to place. However, the current rates of payment under the system of state support (Supplementary Benefit, formerly National Assistance) provide an indicator of what can be regarded as a subsistence standard of living, and several studies have adopted this criterion in assessing the level of hardship among fatherless families, (Finer, 1974; Ministry of Social Security, 1967; Wynn, 1964.) These have shown that the absence of the father dramatically increases the likelihood that a family will become dependent upon state support. Wynn, comparing the proportions receiving assistance in various groups, concluded that 'the absence of the father is more often associated with the dependence of children upon National Assistance than are unemployment, sickness and industrial injury together.' The report on *Circumstances of Families* (1967) estimated that 46 per cent of the fatherless families represented by the sample were in receipt of National Assistance.

Very little information is available concerning the economic position of families in which the mother is absent. George and Wilding (1972) found that 29 per cent of fathers on their own had drawn Supplementary Benefit at some time since the loss of their wives. The Finer Report (1974) estimated that approximately seven per cent of the 100,000 lone fathers in Britain were on Supplementary Benefit in November 1972, and commented that this relatively small proportion made difficult a detailed analysis of the economic circumstances of motherless families in general. It should be pointed out that, apart from Wynn's study, all of the investigations referred to above have dealt with samples of *families* and not *children*, as in the case in our own study. The sampling unit employed will clearly effect the measures obtained, and the extent to which findings from different studies can be compared. For example, the proportion of children living in over-crowded accommodation in England and Wales has been shown to be more than double the proportion of all *persons* in such conditions, (Davie, Butler and Goldstein, 1972).

The present study: family situation and receipt of Supplementary Benefit

During the parental interview carried out when the children in the National Child Development Study were 11, details were obtained of the source of income of each child's family during the preceding 12 months. From this information it was possible to calculate the proportion of children in different family situations whose material welfare had been partially or totally dependent upon state support during the period in question.

Almost half (47 per cent) of the fatherless children in the sample had been dependent upon Supplementary Benefit at some time during the year preceding the follow-up, a finding which corresponds closely with those of the other studies quoted above (table A7.1 (a)). Fatherless children were much more likely than those in motherless families to have received such state support; while the latter in turn contained a significantly higher proportion (13 per cent)[1] than children living with both parents (six per cent).

i) Non-manual and manual groups

Since the likelihood of becoming dependent on state support is higher among manual workers than among those in non-manual occupations, a separate study was made of the figures for each family situation according to social class background.

In cases where the father had had a manual occupation, the same pattern of differences emerged, with just over half (52 per cent) of the fatherless children having received Supplementary Benefit, compared with 18 per cent of the motherless and only seven per cent of those in two-parent families (table A7.1 (c)).

Only 17 of the lone fathers had been in non-manual occupations and none of these had resorted to Supplementary Benefit during the period in question. George and Wilding (1972) have pointed out that the salary levels, nature and conditions of work of these fathers make it easier for them than for manual workers to maintain their employment status following the loss of the mother.

---

1 This figure is considerably lower than that quoted by George and Wilding, probably due in part to sample differences (George and Wilding's sample was drawn largely from social welfare agencies), and in part to differences in the time periods involved. George and Wilding's figure referred to receipt of Supplementary Benefit at some time since loss of mother and 40 per cent had been alone for four years or more.

Among the two-parent families in which the father had had a non-manual job only two per cent had received Supplementary Benefit (table A7.1 (b)). The figure for fatherless families, however, was 31 per cent, so that it would seem that the risk of becoming dependent upon state support is enormously increased by the loss of the father, irrespective of the family's social class background. The relative *change* as well as the actual *level* of income is likely to be an important determinant of a family's sense of hardship and deprivation, and this in turn may influence their morale and ability to adapt to, and cope with, drastically changed circumstances. The parents' own, more subjective, attitude to their financial situation will be discussed later.

ii) Cause of family situation

Among the motherless children there was little relationship between the cause of the family breakdown and dependence upon Supplementary Benefit, although the numbers involved were very small. In contrast, among the fatherless children, the circumstances which had led to the father's absence did seem to be closely linked to the family's subsequent economic situation. Although receipt of Supplementary Benefit was more common among each fatherless group than among the two-parent children, those whose father had died were much less likely to have been dependent on such support (25 per cent) than children who were illegitimate (48 per cent) or whose parents' marriage had broken down (61 per cent) (table A7.1 (a)).

It was interesting to find that among the children whose fathers had died there was a relatively small difference in receipt of Supplementary Benefit between those in non-manual and manual homes. (Twenty per cent and 25 per cent respectively had recieved such support.) Children living with divorced and separated mothers however, showed a marked difference in dependence on Supplementary Benefit according to their social class. Thirty-nine per cent of those from non-manual homes had received benefit compared with 69 per cent of those from a manual background. No doubt the lower overall rate of dependence among widows reflects the provision of the Widowed Mother's Allowance, which would not differ greatly between the two social class groups. Maintenance from a former husband following marital breakdown on the other hand is likely to be a less reliable and less substantial income, especially among the manual groups, and this was no doubt reflected in the very high proportion of these families who had been dependent upon Supplementary Benefit.

The fact that children from manual backgrounds who were cared for by divorced and separated mothers showed by far the highest rate of dependency on Supplementary Benefit (69 per cent) may tie in with the findings reported in Chapter Six that this group contained the highest proportion of large families (38 per cent came from families with four or more children). The greater the number of children, the more likely it would be that Supplementary Benefit payments would exceed the mother's potential earnings, while the costs and problems of arranging substitute day care for a large number of children would be a further disincentive to employment.

Supplementary Benefit as the sole source of income

Much has been written of the depressing, undermining effects upon male heads of households of prolonged reliance on state support. Little is known about the psychological and social effects of such a situation upon women who are bringing up families alone. What can be said with certainty, however, is that long-term dependence on Supplementary Benefit means long-term hardship. In spite of the provision of a 'long-term additional allowance', the level of benefit provides for little more than the basic essentials of day-to-day living and precludes any real build-up of resources to cover such important items as household repairs and re-decorations, furniture, clothes and holidays.

An examination was made of the number of children in different family situations whose parents claimed to have had no source of income other than Supplementary Benefit during the twelve month period in question. From this it appeared that only 29 (0.2 per cent) of the children in two-parent families and just one of the 97 motherless children in the sample had been in this situation (table S7.2). As far as the fatherless children were concerned, however, it was found that no fewer than one in six (17 per cent) had been totally dependent on Supplementary Benefit for their material support during the previous year. Children of widows were again the least vulnerable in this respect (only 2 per cent were in this situation) but the figures for children of marital breakdown were one in four (24 per cent), and for those who were illegitimate almost one in every three (30 per cent).

Family situation and receipt of free school meals

During the interview with the health visitor, parents were asked whether any child of the family was currently receiving free meals at school, and this information provided a further indication of the level of income among families of children in the sample. Families receiving Supplementary Benefit automatically qualify for free school meals, but others are also entitled to this benefit if their net income falls below a certain level (although not all necessarily receive it). Thus, one would expect to find that the proportion of families receiving free meals would be somewhat higher than the proportion receiving Supplementary·Benefit, and this was found to be the case.

The findings also showed, however, that the pattern of differences between the various family groups was very similar to that which emerged where receipt of Supplementary Benefit was examined. Motherless children were twice as likely, and fatherless children almost eight times as likely, to have had free meals as their counterparts in complete families (table A.7.3 (a)). The figure for fatherless children (60 per cent) was rather higher than that found in the government survey *Circumstances of Families* (52 per cent), which, however involved a sample of *families*, not one of *children* as in the present study.

i) Non-manual and manual groups

As was the case with receipt of Supplementary Benefit, the difference in the proportion of fatherless and two-parent children receiving free meals was marked at both social class levels (tables A7.3 (b) and A7.3 (c)). Motherless children, too remained more likely to have had free meals than their peers in two-parent families when those from manual homes were studied separately.

ii) Cause of family situation

Among the motherless families, there was no relationship between the cause of the mothers' absence and the proportion of children receiving free school meals. Looking at the fatherless, however, it appeared that by far the highest number receiving free school meals was found in families broken by divorce, separation or desertion — more than two-thirds of all the children in this group, and as many as four out of five of those from lower social class homes.

Rather surprisingly, in view of the differences when Supplementary Benefit was examined, the proportions of illegitimate and widow's children receiving free meals were very similar. It would seem less likely that this reflected a comparable level of income in the two groups than a lower level of take-up of free meals among illegitimate children, possibly due to lack of knowledge about eligibility, or to differences in attitudes among these families.

Although only a small difference had been found in the proportions of widows' children from non-manual and manual backgrounds who were dependent upon Supplementary Benefit, these two groups differed much more markedly when receipt of free school meals was examined. While this may reflect social class differences in the level of take-up of this benefit, it also suggests predictable differences in the income level of the two groups which were masked when Supplementary Benefit was the income measure used. It is perhaps worth noting at this point that simple dichotomies such as those employed here represent a fairly crude measure of resources and that the results quoted should be treated with some caution.

Although a relatively high proportion (60 per cent) of fatherless children were receiving free meals, it should not be assumed that the remainder would not have been entitled to this benefit and were living in families whose resources were substantially greater, for there is evidence (e.g. Lynes, 1972) that a considerable proportion of eligible families do not in fact take up means-tested benefits. Marsden (1969) estimated that one-third of the children in his sample were not taking free meals, although their dependence on Supplementary Benefit automatically entitled them to do so. 'It appeared that some families paid for their meals, while in others children came home rather than face the stigma of taking free dinners.' Marsden cautiously points out that the influence of stigma is difficult to estimate, but other writers (e.g. Kay 1972) have commented on the unnecessarily humiliating and offensive singling out which frequently characterizes the administration of means-tested benefits such as free school meals. It would seem not unlikely that such embarrassment would be doubly painful to a child already 'different' by virtue of his abnormal family circumstances.

Feelings of financial hardship

The two areas studied so far, Supplementary Benefit and free school meals, give an objective, if rather crude, assessment of the number of children in the National Child Development Study sample who were supported on very limited financial resources. However, it is important to consider also how the families concerned *felt* about their financial situation, for such subjective feelings would doubtless play an important part in determining the effects of a family's economic circumstances upon its morale, resilience and ability to cope.

During the interview each parent was asked: 'Have you been seriously troubled by financial hardship in the past twelve months?'. The responses to such a question would obviously depend to some extent on the attitudes and frames of reference of the individuals concerned. For example, the widow who had previously enjoyed the security and comfort based on a husband's high wage or salary may have experienced a sense of serious deprivation when forced to rely upon state support or her own limited earning capacity. On the other hand, the separated mother who had struggled to support a family on the inadequate and erratic contributions of a recalcitrant husband may have felt that even the limited income provided by Supplementary Benefit represented a welcome improvement in security.

The actual level of income was also likely to play a part, of course, and in order to reduce the range of income levels involved, it was decided to confine the analysis of perceived hardship to families whose children had received free school meals.[1]

---

1 Motherless families were excluded from this analysis as only 16 had received free school meals.

Perhaps the most striking finding to emerge from this analysis was the high proportion of parents who felt that they had *not* been seriously troubled by financial hardship, even though their low income entitled their children to free school meals. More than half (51 per cent) of the two-parent families, and 40 per cent of the fatherless gave a negative answer when asked if they had been troubled in this way (table S7.4). This finding should perhaps serve as a caution to attaching too much weight to answers to such a subjective question, although the marked variations in response between different family groups which are described below are of considerable interest, even if they reflect little more than differences in interpretation of the question.

Feelings of hardship or deprivation will depend to a large extent upon the attitudes, expectations and previous experience of the persons concerned, and so it seems likely that different factors played a part in the responses of the various groups. For many of the two-parent families it might be that low income and limited resources were a long-term and long-accepted fact of life. Thus, for the parent resigned to a continuous struggle to make ends meet, perhaps nothing less than a major financial crisis would be regarded as bringing 'serious financial hardship'.

For most of the unsupported mothers, on the other hand, the loss of the partner would have entailed a drop in the family's income. The absence of the male head of household is almost bound to mean a sharp reduction in income, as our own follow-up study has shown, (Ferri and Robinson, 1976).

The contrast, then, between the income received as a complete family, and that obtainable by an unsupported parent, may lead to a greater sense of hardship and deprivation among these families than among unbroken families whose level of income as defined here is likely to be very similar.[1]

i) Cause of family situation

Even within the restricted income range of the groups examined, mothers on their own were more likely to claim that they had suffered hardship than were their counterparts in unbroken families. Within the fatherless group however, the situation was complicated by a marked variation in response between widows and mothers whose marriage had broken down. Only 40 per cent of the widows claimed to have faced serious financial hardship, compared with 70 per cent of the divorced, separated or deserted mothers. These two groups, in fact, contained

---

1   Although there would clearly be a variation in actual income levels within this broadly defined category of families receiving free school meals, it is unlikely that income differences between the various family situations could account for the highly significant differences in perceived hardship.

respectively the lowest and highest proportions who said they had felt such hardship. What factors could account for such a difference? In particular, why should such a *low* proportion of widows have felt troubled financially — for this is surely a more surprising figure than the 70 per cent found among divorced/separated mothers?

It seems likely that the discrepancy reflected differences in the circumstances and experiences of widowed mothers and those whose marriage had broken down. Although the *level* of income of the two groups was broadly similar, the *source* of that income was different and this may well have affected their attitudes and outlook. Most widowed mothers receive a Widowed Mother's Allowance as of right, and are free to boost their income through part-time earnings without any deduction being made from this allowance. This is likely to be seen as a more socially acceptable source of income than the Supplementary Benefit upon which so many divorced and separated mothers were dependent, and which precluded more than token part-time earnings without corresponding reduction of benefit. The feelings of stigma attached to reliance on non-contributory state support and the oft-quoted unsympathetic and even hostile attitudes displayed by some administrative officials may have combined to produce in these mothers a greater sense of deprivation and resentment. Marsden, (1969), investigating feelings of deprivation among his sample of unsupported mothers on National Assistance, wrote that some 'embraced the suggestion that they were deprived as a criticism of their children's fathers and the National Assistance Board'. This quotation suggests a further possible explanation of the difference between widows and others, namely, that the circumstances of the family breakdown might result in widows being less ready than divorced, separated or deserted mothers to acknowledge financial hardship which was directly attributable to the loss of their partner. Again, it may also be the case that feelings of hardship relate not only to actual income level but to other material factors, such as housing, an area in which, as a later chapter will show, widows were also in an advantageous position compared to other unsupported mothers.

Summary and conclusions

Evidence from the present study showing the relatively high proportion of one-parent, especially fatherless, families receiving Supplementary Benefit and free school meals confirms the findings of other investigators that the absence of a parent has a seriously damaging effect on the family's material resources. It has also been shown that, apart from widowed mothers, fatherless families were more likely to *feel* troubled by financial hardship, even when compared with two-parent families whose income was similarly limited.

In terms of the measures adopted here, fatherless families were harder hit economically than those in which the mother was the absent parent. Among the fatherless themselves, there were also differences in resources according to the reason for the family breakdown; widows' families tended to be less dependent upon Supplementary Benefit and free school meals than other fatherless families, and were also less likely to *feel* seriously troubled by their financial situation. Such findings are in line with those of other investigators (Catholic Housing Aid Society 1967; Department of Health and Social Security, 1972; Hunt *et al.*, 1973; Kriesberg, 1971; Marsden, 1969). The Department of Health and Social Security report on *Families receiving Supplementary Benefit* (1972) found that widows contained by far the lowest proportion with 'income less than basic need', while in the United States, Kriesberg reported that, 'widows and their children make up a shrinking proportion of fatherless families receiving public assistance'.

In spite of these variations between different groups of one-parent families it should perhaps be emphasized that they are only differences in the *degree* of disadvantage suffered by families which lack a parent, and that the findings reported here leave little doubt that children in *all* types of one-parent family are economically handicapped when compared with their peers in two-parent homes. As Marsden (1969) has pointed out in commenting on the relatively favourable treatment accorded to widows in social security legislation — 'measured against standards of living in the community, provision for widows is still inadequate.'

How many children in one-parent families are poor? It is impossible to give an accurate figure from the available data; more than half of the children concerned were receiving free meals, yet, for the reasons suggested earlier, this almost certainly underestimates the number supported on such low incomes. Evidence from the follow-up study (Ferri and Robinson, 1976) showed that hardship in one-parent families was frequently associated with low earnings as well as with dependence on official support, and that this was the case among motherless as well as fatherless families. The Finer Report (1974) estimated that as many as 15 per cent of fatherless families *not* receiving Supplementary Benefit were actually living *below* Supplementary Benefit level. It seems not unreasonable to suggest that a substantial majority of one-parent children in the present sample had experienced a standard of living which was seriously depressed by lack of resources.

It is hardly necessary to spell out in detail what life on a subsistence income can mean for children in our present day society. Not only may the basic needs of food, clothing and adequate housing be lacking, but also the opportunity to participate in the play and social activities which form such a vital part of the developing child's environment and experience. As Margaret Wynn (1964) put it: 'A subsistence income is inadequate to provide a satisfactory childhood'. The burden of continuing financial hardship and the inability to maintain a standard of living comparable to that of other families are likely to produce feelings of frustration and resentment in parents and children alike. For the members of a family which loses a parent, re-integration and absorption into the community through extra-familial activities are likely to be particularly important and beneficial, yet such participation may be precluded by the lack of resources which characterize the one-parent situation. The effects of a low income are thus far-reaching — as Blake (1972) pointed out when describing *The Plight of One-Parent Families*: 'Poverty affects them in every sphere of their lives and also accentuates their isolation, so that the two cannot be considered separately.'

Chapter Eight

Employment and the lone parent

The findings reported in the last chapter have shown that the absence of a parent presents a serious economic threat to a family, and that one of the major problems facing a mother or father bringing up children singlehanded lies in obtaining an adequate income. In the absence of a private income or a generous pension or maintenance allowance, lone parents of either sex are faced with the choice of going out to work and making alternative child care arrangements, or becoming dependent upon state aid and remaining at home to look after their children themselves. Although it would appear that lone mothers and fathers face the same problem of combining these two full-time tasks, it is society's expectation that men should give priority to their bread-winning role, while women should put their home-making and child-rearing responsibilities first, at least when the children are very young (McKay, George and Wilding, 1972). This means that fathers and mothers left on their own are likely to approach the problem from two different standpoints. In studying the employment situation of lone parents, therefore, an examination was made of the number of unsupported mothers who had taken up work, while as far as the fathers were concerned, our interest focussed on the level of unemployment among fathers on their own and those in 'complete' families.

Working mothers

The last few decades have witnessed a marked increase in the proportion of married women workers in the labour force (Hunt, 1968). Not all of these will be mothers of course, although Klein (1965), in her study of working wives, found that half of the sample concerned had children under fifteen years of age.

There are several factors which may motivate a mother to take up work outside the home. First, there are economic pressures to boost the family income, either in order to make ends meet or to afford the increasing number of goods and services which a consumer-oriented society translates from luxuries into necessities. Then there are psychological and social reasons why a mother may wish to take up or return to work. The companionship and social interaction of an office, shop or factory may be a welcome alternative to the lonely routine of housework and the company of children, while the gradual change in the social position and expectations of women has resulted in fewer being willing to confine their role to that of housewife and mother.

However, while there are some forces which encourage a mother to go out to work, there are others which act as disincentives. The job opportunities open to women are still relatively limited and in spite of the trend towards equal pay, women's earnings remain well below those of men (Pinder, 1969). Another major problem facing the working mother is that of making satisfactory arrangements for the care of her children. Depending upon her working hours, substitute care may be required for the whole day for pre-school children, while older children may need supervision during the hours before and/or after school. The rise in the proportion of married women working has not been accompanied by a corresponding increase in official day care provision, and available estimates suggest that only a small proportion of children of working mothers are protected by any kind of public supervision (Wynn, 1964).

Employment and the unsupported mother

The same kind of considerations as those discussed above are likely to influence the unsupported mother's attitude towards employment. The difference in the situation of these mothers and that of their counterparts in two-parent homes is rather one of degree; for in almost every sphere the pressures on the lone mother are more severe — and consequently more conflicting. The financial problems facing a fatherless family are such that the mother may feel that she has no choice but to go out to work. Whereas in a two-parent family, the mother's earnings can normally be regarded as a useful supplement to the family income, the wages of a mother on her own may well constitute the major, or even the sole source of financial support for herself and her children. However, the extent to which a lone mother's employment is a viable source of income will depend upon her earning power. Low wages, combined with the extra *costs* of working in terms of day care provision, transport, insurance, extra clothing and the need to buy expensive convenience foods may well reduce the financial advantages of full-time employment to negligible proportions. If, on the other hand, a mother becomes dependent upon Supplementary Benefit for the support of her family, her ability to boost this income through part-time work is restricted by the 'earnings rule'. This states that part-time earnings in excess of £2[1] per week will be accompanied by a corresponding reduction in benefit. The incentive to take up employment is thus drastically reduced for all except those who can earn a wage or salary sufficiently in excess of Supplementary Benefit rates to cover the extra costs of working and still make employment financially worthwhile.

While the economic incentives to work may thus be less obvious than the needs of fatherless families would seem to suggest, the social aspects of employment may be particularly important to mothers on their own. The difficulties such mothers may face in establishing social contacts and becoming re-integrated into groups outside the family may be greatly eased by involvement in a work situation. As the Catholic Housing Aid Society (1972) has pointed out, mothers on their own are 'isolated and lonely, and going to work reduces this isolation . . . The measure of independence that results from a weekly wage, the increase in self-respect and self-help are factors which contribute to healing the scars of marriage breakdown.'

Given the pressing financial needs which may oblige an unsupported mother to go out to work, the problem of making suitable day care arrangements for her children may be correspondingly intensified. Although most day nurseries give priority to children from one-parent homes, the totally inadequate overall provision means that only a minority of such children can be catered for in this way. Holman (1970) found that one in four of the unsupported mothers in his study who had applied for a day nursery place for their children had failed to obtain one. Wynn (1964) estimated that only one in three fatherless children under five with mothers in employment were cared for with public supervision. Under such circumstances many mothers may be obliged to accept care arrangements which they themselves regard as inadequate and unsatisfactory (Yudkin and Holme, 1963). Apart from exerting directly harmful effects upon the children, such a situation could result in feelings of guilt and anxiety which may be damaging to mother and children alike.

The unsupported mother thus seems to be subject to conflicting forces with regard to employment, some motivating her to take up work, others placing considerable obstacles in the way of her doing so. As Carlier Mackiewicz (1969) pointed out in her study of widows in France, these mothers 'find themselves in a situation where the utmost necessity and the impossibility of taking up employment coincide.'[2]

---

1   £4 per week from November 1975.
2   Author's translation.

In spite of these conflicting influences, all the available evidence suggests that the pressures to work in fact outweigh the obstacles, and that unsupported mothers are more likely to be employed than mothers in complete families. Rowntree (1955) found that one in every two of the lone mothers of her sample of four-year-old children were working compared with only about one in six of the mothers in 'stable' homes. The national survey quoted in the Plowden Report (1967) showed that 57 per cent of the unsupported mothers of seven, eight and eleven-year-old children were employed, as against 38 per cent of those in two-parent families. Similar findings have emerged from studies carried out in the United States. (Kriesberg, 1970; Nye and Hoffman, 1963).

The present study: family situation and number of mothers working

When the children in our study were eleven, information concerning the mothers' employment situation was obtained during the parental interview. Mothers were asked whether they had been engaged in full-time or part-time (under 30 hours a week) employment at any time during the preceding twelve months. Full details were also obtained about the nature of the mothers' most recent job, and also of the number of hours she spent away from home outside the normal school day (i.e. 9 a.m. to 4 p.m.).

An analysis of the information obtained showed a higher level of employment among unsupported mothers (62 per cent) than among those in two-parent families (57 per cent) (table A8.1 (a)). This difference was quite small, however, and was largely due to the relatively high proportion of widows who had worked during the year in question (67 per cent). The level of employment among mothers whose marriage had broken down (59 per cent) or whose children were illegitimate (60 per cent) was very similar to that of the mothers in two-parent homes. However, the family's social class background was found to be of importance here. At the non-manual level, the employment rate of widows (64 per cent) and divorced and separated mothers (63 per cent) was practically identical, and higher than that of mothers in 'complete' families (49 per cent) (table A8.1 (b)). Among those from manual backgrounds on the other hand, the divorced and separated were no more likely to have worked (59 per cent) than their counterparts in two-parent families (60 per cent); it was only the widows who contained a comparatively high proportion in employment (71 per cent) (table A8.1 (c)).

i) Full-time and part-time work

An examination was also made of the *type* of work, i.e. full or part-time, which had been undertaken by the mothers concerned. This showed rather more marked differences between the unsupported mothers and the rest. Of the mothers who had worked, only one in three of those in two-parent families had had full-time jobs, compared with more than half of the mothers on their own. No doubt these differences reflect the relative financial pressures on the two groups, with the former having greater freedom to choose part-time jobs which would be more compatible with their family responsibilities. There was no difference in this respect between widows and divorced or separated mothers; in each case approximately half of those who worked had had full-time jobs. This figure rose to three-quarters, however, among mothers of illegitimate children.

Contrary to the findings concerning the overall numbers in employment, social class background was *not* found to be associated with the relative levels of full and part-time work among the different groups of mothers.

The findings reported here are somewhat surprising in the light of those of other studies which have compared the work patterns of mothers in one and two-parent families. Firstly, the overall difference in the employment level of the two groups was much smaller than that reported elsewhere (Plowden, 1967; Rowntree, 1955). This may to some extent reflect a 'levelling up' on the part of mothers in unbroken families as the proportion of married women in employment continues to rise. The fact that the children in the present sample were rather older than those in the studies mentioned above is also likely to be associated with a relatively high level of employment among mothers in 'normal' family circumstances.

Secondly, the comparatively high proportion of working widows contrasts sharply with the findings of other investigations which have consistently shown widows to be *less* likely to work than other unsupported mothers. (Carlier Mackiewicz 1969; Plowden 1967; Rowntree 1955; Siegel *et al.* 1963).

ii) Cause of family situation

The present figures would seem to suggest a relatively *low* level of employment among divorced and separated mothers rather than a particularly *high* level among widows, at least among those from manual backgrounds. One would expect to find that mothers from manual homes were more likely to work than those from a non-manual background and among widows and mothers in two-parent families, this was indeed the case. The same did *not* hold true, however, for mothers who were divorced or separated.

As mentioned earlier, the factors involved in a mother's decision to work or not are likely to be numerous and complex, and without further information it is difficult to offer more than a tentative explanation of these rather unexpected findings. However, there are several points which may go some way towards accounting for the difference reported here between the widows and the mothers whose marriage had broken down.

First of all, as far as part-time work was concerned, mothers in receipt of Supplementary Benefit were subject to the earnings rule referred to above, which virtually destroyed any financial incentive to take a job, and, as Chapter Seven showed, as many as 69 per cent of the divorced or separated mothers from manual homes had received Supplementary Benefit during the year in question. The Widowed Mothers' Allowance on the other hand is not subject to any such restriction on part-time earnings and so part-time work was a much more viable economic proposition for widows than it was for lone mothers who were dependent upon Supplementary Benefit.

With regard to full-time work, the main problem facing the lone mother is that of earning enough to lift the family income sufficiently high above the Supplementary Benefit level to make employment worth the extra costs and problems which it entails, and this would clearly be an impossible target for many of the mothers involved here. Another important factor in this context is family size. Other investigators (e.g. Kriesberg, 1970) have found a strong association between employment and number of children among unsupported mothers, for while state benefits increase with the number of children in a family, income from earnings does not. It was seen in Chapter Six that divorced or separated mothers from manual homes were more likely than widows to have large families of four or more children. A further analysis which took account of family size showed that, where there were only one or two children, both widows *and* divorced or separated mothers had a higher employment rate than mothers in complete families (tables S8.2 (a) (b) (c)). Among families with three or more children, however, only the widows showed a slightly higher proportion who had worked.[1] The problems of finding substitute day care is also likely to be increased for the mother of a large family, and even when suitable arrangements can be made, the additional cost would further reduce the financial return from employment.

The age of the children concerned will also be relevant to the question of the need for substitute care. It was shown in Chapter Six that widows tended to be considerably older than divorced or separated mothers, so it would be less likely that their families included very young children. This would mean fewer day care problems for widows than for divorced or separated mothers who wished to take up work,

---

1 The association between family size and employment was even more marked among mothers of illegitimate children, although small numbers in this group made comparisons difficult.

and may have been a further contributory factor to the different levels of employment in the two groups.

What kind of jobs?

What sort of work do mothers on their own take up? It has already been suggested that, for many mothers, a job must be sufficiently remunerative to exceed the income obtainable from Supplementary Benefit. On the other hand, the problems and pressures facing an unsupported mother are such that her employment opportunities are likely to be severely restricted.

In order to throw some light on this rather complex question, a comparison was made of the actual occupations in which the different groups of mothers had most recently been employed. In doing so, the mother's educational level was taken into account, since this would clearly be related to the type of employment for which she would be qualified. It was found that mothers on their own were less likely to have stayed at school after the minimum leaving age than those in two parent families (19 per cent compared with 26 per cent) (table S8.3). Because of the rather small numbers involved, the comparisons were confined to the proportion of mothers who had had high status (professional, managerial or 'intermediate'[1]) jobs, and those who had been employed in low status (manual) occupations.

Some interesting differences were found among the mothers who had stayed at school beyond the minimum leaving age[2] (Table S8.4 (a)). Divorced or separated mothers were twice as likely as those in two-parent families to have had manual occupations (26 per cent as against 13 per cent), while only half as many had obtained high status jobs (17 per cent and 33 per cent respectively). On the other hand, as far as widows were concerned, the trend was in the opposite direction — 42 per cent had had professional/managerial/intermediate jobs and only eight per cent had been in manual employment, and the difference between widows and divorced or separated mothers reached statistical significance.

A similar, although less marked, pattern emerged among mothers who had left school at the earliest opportunity (Table S8.4 (b)). Very few mothers in any family situation had obtained high status jobs, but more than half (52 per cent) of the divorced or separated mothers were found to have had manual jobs compared with 44 per cent of widows and 40 per cent of mothers in two-parent homes.

The classification of educational level employed here is clearly a crude one and may well have masked considerable differences in

1   According to the Registrar General's 1966 Classification of Occupations
2   Because of small numbers (8) mothers of illegitimate children were excluded.

qualifications between the various groups of mothers involved. Yet it seems unlikely that such differences could wholly account for the marked trends revealed here, and it is possible that the findings reflect, at least in part, the different attitudes adopted by society at large towards various groups of lone mothers which were referred to in Chapter One. The general sympathy shown to widows might not only facilitate their entry into superior employment situations, but, although empirical evidence is totally lacking, might also award them priority in access to the scarce facilities for re-training. The less sympathetic attitudes adopted towards divorced, separated or unmarried mothers on the other hand, may perhaps have penalized them in the labour market and further restricted the already limited opportunities available to them in their disadvantaged situation.

Number of hours away from home

We have now seen that unsupported mothers were more likely to work, more likely to work full-time, and, with the exception of widows, more likely to have less remunerative and prestigious jobs. As one of the chief problems facing any working mother is the day care of her children, it was felt important to discover how many hours each day our different groups of mothers were absent from home. Information was available on the total number of hours each mother was away outside the normal school day (9 a.m. to 4 p.m.). Looking first at those who had worked full-time showed that while 23 per cent of mothers in two-parent families had had jobs which appeared to coincide with the child's school day, the figure dropped to 14 per cent among unsupported mothers (Table S8.5 (a)). At the other extreme, 21 per cent of the two-parent and 30 per cent of the unsupported mothers were absent from home for three hours or more outside the school day. Mothers of illegitimate children were the most likely to be away for long periods — over three-quarters of these were absent for two hours or more outside 9 a.m. to 4 p.m.

As far as the mothers who had had part-time jobs were concerned, there were no differences according to family circumstances in the number of hours which they spent away from home (Table S8.5 (b)). What was striking, however, was the fact that part-time work did *not* on the whole appear to coincide with the hours the children spent at school. Almost half of all the mothers who worked part-time were away from home for some time outside the hours 9 a.m. and 4 p.m., and one in every three was absent for two hours or more. It would clearly be wrong, therefore, to assume that part-time work presents an automatic solution to the problems of combining employment with the care of children.

The above findings indicated that, in all family situations, a substantial proportion of working mothers were away from home for some time outside the school day. As far as the two-parent families were concerned it might well have been the case that fathers were at home during all or part of the mothers' absence, for example when mothers worked 'twilight shifts'. For mothers on their own, however, the situation was inevitably different. Without further information it was not possible to say whether the absence from home of unsupported mothers who went out to work meant that they had succeeded in making satisfactory alternative child care arrangements or whether their children were likely to be left to fend for themselves. However, in view of the pressures on lone mothers to go out to work in spite of the difficulties of providing for their children, it would be over-optimistic to suggest that the former explanation reflects the reality of the situation. It seems more likely that many lone mothers had been obliged to accept employment conditions which conflicted with the day care needs of their children. Under such circumstances, it would not be surprising to find that the substitute care arrangements made for the children were, in many cases, unsatisfactory or even non-existent.

Unemployment and the lone father

As pointed out at the beginning of this chapter, society looks askance at the father who gives up work to care for his children, thereby becoming dependent upon state aid. Fathers are not 'expected' to take on the task of bringing up children singlehanded, and our social system is not geared towards helping them to do so. Cases have even been cited (Ferri and Robinson, 1976) in which the only 'solution' offered by the social services to a father left on his own is that his children be taken into care.

If a lone father is to remain in employment he has to make arrangements for his children to be looked after. Our own follow-up study and that of George and Wilding (1972) found that relatives, rather than any official agencies, were the chief source of assistance in this respect. Such help however, is clearly not available to all and, as the above studies have suggested, may be a less than ideal arrangement even when it is.

For some fathers, the only possible course of action if the family is to remain together is to stop work and take on the care of home and children themselves. Twenty-nine per cent of the fathers in George and Wilding's study were found to have given up employment at some time since the loss of their wives, and the recent report on 'Families and their needs' (Hunt *et al.* 1973) also found that a relatively high proportion of lone fathers were not working.

During the interview with parents in the present study, details were collected of any period of unemployment which the fathers had experienced in the preceding twelve months. The information obtained showed that one in six of the lone fathers had been out of work at some stage, compared with only one in fourteen of the fathers in two parent families (Table A8.6 (a)). A separate analysis of those in manual occupations showed that this discrepancy could not be explained by differences in social class background (Table A8.6 (b)).

Although the numbers involved were very small, it appeared that fathers on their own not only showed a higher unemployment rate but were more likely to have been out of work for a long time. The proportion who had been without a job for six months or more was five times greater among the lone fathers than among those in unbroken families.

No details were available concerning the circumstances which had led to the unemployment of the fathers in the sample, so that it could not be established whether the figures reflected 'voluntary' unemployment on the part of fathers with a dual role to fulfil, or whether their family responsibilities had made them less reliable employees and thus more vulnerable to dismissal or redundancy. As was the case with mothers on their own, the lower the earning power of a lone father, and the more his job involves long, irregular hours which are incompatible with his domestic responsibilities, the less incentive he has to continue in employment rather than become dependent upon state aid. George and Wilding (1972) showed in their study how much easier it was for fathers in middle class, salaried occupations to dovetail their earnings and caring roles without an unacceptable loss of income. For a father in a manual occupation, the requirements of shift work, the inflexibility of the actual work situation and the frequent dependence on overtime for an adequate income may well mean that the demands of home and work become irreconcilable.

Summary and conclusions

We have shown in this chapter that the work patterns of the unsupported mothers in our sample differed somewhat from that of mothers in complete families, both in the likelihood of being employed and in the nature and conditions of the jobs which they undertook. In every respect the mother on her own seemed to be at a disadvantage, although differences according to the cause of the one-parent situation made the picture less than clear-cut. The relatively high level of employment among widows appeared to reflect the greater financial incentive to work which freedom from the earnings rule allowed them, whilst most other unsupported mothers seemed to have little opportunity .to achieve more than a subsistence income whether they went out to work or not.

But what about the effects on her children of a mother going out to work? This has long been a controversial issue, and the rise in the number of married women working has been viewed with alarm by many who claim that maternal employment has an adverse effect on wide-ranging aspects of young children's welfare and development. These claims, however, are based more upon assumptions than upon solid evidence, for numerous investigations in this field have failed to produce a clear consensus. As Stolz (1960) concluded: 'one can say almost anything one desires about the children of employed mothers and support the statement by some research study'. In a later review of research in this area, Wallston (1973) found the situation still somewhat confused, and cited a number of studies which showed that the relationship between maternal employment and children's development varied according to social class background, attitudes and behaviour of the mother and the sex of the child.

The analysis of the information collected for the National Child Development Study (Davie, Bulter and Goldstein, 1972) has recently put the problem into some perspective. This showed that children whose mothers had worked before they started school had slightly lower scores in reading and arithmetic at seven years of age, and were seen as slightly less well-adjusted than children whose mothers had not worked. If the mother worked *after* the child started school the differences were even smaller and only apparent in the case of reading and social adjustment. Compared with the relationship between such outcomes and other factors, such as social class, the difference in children's performance due to their mothers' working or not was very small, and as a result the authors concluded that 'many of the accusations laid at the door of the working mother are ill-founded'.

This analysis, however, was confined to children who were living with both natural parents, and it would clearly be rash to extend its findings to the one-parent situation. It might in fact be hypothesized that the absence from home due to employment of the sole remaining parent would be more damaging to a child who already has to cope with distressing family circumstances. It was felt important therefore, to take account of the mothers' employment status when comparing the school attainment and social adjustment of children in different family situations (see Chapters Twelve and Thirteen).

Very few studies have looked at the effects of maternal employment in the fatherless family, but those which exist have produced some interesting, and perhaps rather surprising, findings. Nye (1957) found that while there was a positive association between delinquency and mother working among families where both parents were present, there was *no* such relationship in a comparable sample of fatherless homes. His findings also showed that fatherless children whose mothers were employed displayed fewer psychosomatic symptoms and enjoyed 'a closer affectional relationship' with their mothers than those whose mothers had remained at home.

Kriesberg's (1970) study provides some indirect evidence in this area by showing that unsupported mothers who were employed had higher educational aspirations for their children than those who did not work, although he also points out that the mothers' work commitments prevented them from displaying their concern through involvement in school affairs and contact with teachers; a point which should perhaps be borne in mind when considering teachers' assessments of parental interest.

Although the above findings are fragmentary and inconclusive, they do suggest that certain personality and social factors may be of importance in a study of working mothers and the effects of maternal employment upon children. It may be that, in the case of fatherless families, mothers who do decide to work tend to be those with the most resilience and energy and the greatest determination to overcome the disadvantaged position in which their family circumstances have placed them.

In view of the paucity of studies of motherless families it is hardly surprising that there is no evidence available about the effects upon children of a lone father continuing to work or remaining at home to care for his family. Unfortunately, the number of unemployed fathers in the present sample was too small to be treated as a separate group for the purposes of such an evaluation. However, it is well-established that prolonged unemployment has a demoralizing effect upon a man's self-image, and can lead to a vicious circle of apathy and depression which make re-employment increasingly difficult. The potentially damaging effect when this is combined with the stresses and problems facing fathers on their own, might be particularly severe, with the victims being not only the fathers themselves but also the children whose welfare has become their total responsibility.

Chapter Nine

The housing situation of children in one-parent families

The widespread and often acute housing problems to be found in many areas of this country have been highlighted in recent years by a number of official reports (Milner Holland, 1965; Cullingworth, 1969; Francis, 1971; Greve, 1971). The problem is a two-fold one: on the one hand the insufficient total supply of housing is evidenced by the growing number of people officially designated 'homeless', while on the other hand, the inferior and unacceptable standard of much of the existing housing stock is reflected in the large number of households reported as lacking some of the most basic essentials such as hot water, a fixed bath and an indoor toilet. (OPCS General Household Survey, 1971).

Where such problems exist, it is not surprising to find that particular sections of the community, for example the old, the sick, the unemployed and immigrant groups, are especially vulnerable to the hardship which they bring. One-parent families are no exception to this, and the difficulties which many of them face in finding and keeping suitable accommodation is a recurring theme in studies of such groups. Holman (1970), reporting the high level of house and amenity sharing among his sample of unsupported mothers, commented that 'even when compared with other sections of society suffering from adverse housing, the lone mothers ... came off badly.' The Finer Report (1974) concluded that housing was the 'largest single problem of one-parent families', and that this problem was 'second only to financial difficulties and to a large extent exacerbated by them.'

When the children in the present study were eleven, a great deal of information about their housing situation was obtained during the course of the parental interview. This included details of the type of accommodation lived in, the form of tenure held, the availability of basic amenities, the level of overcrowding, the number of study children sharing their beds and the number of times the family had moved home since the study child's birth. In addition, parents were asked to say whether or not they were satisfied with the accommodation in which the family was currently living.

For each of the factors mentioned above, comparisons were made between children in the different groups of fatherless and motherless families and those living with both parents. As social class background had been shown to be related to factors in the housing situation when the children were aged seven (Davie, Butler and Goldstein, 1972), separate analyses were carried out for children from non-manual and manual homes.[1] In order to simplify the reporting of the findings however, the results of these analyses will be described only when they produced results inconsistent with those from the overall comparisons.

Type of accommodation

The first question concerning the housing conditions of the children in the sample was; 'In what *kind* of accommodation were these 11-year-olds living?' The findings showed that the great majority of children in all types of family had a whole house at their disposal, although a sizeable minority lived in a flat (or maisonette) and a small proportion in rooms or a caravan.

While no sweeping generalizations can be made about the relative merits or disadvantages of house or flat dwelling, it seems reasonable to suppose that a house, especially one with a garden or yard, is on the whole a preferable type of accommodation for a family with young children. Comparing the numbers in different parental situations whose families were occupying a whole house showed a marked difference between fatherless children (78 per cent) and those living with both parents (91 per cent) (Table S9.1). However, looking at the three fatherless groups separately, it appeared that widows' children did not in fact differ from those in two-parent families. On the other hand, 23 per cent of the children who were fatherless due to marital breakdown lived in a flat or maisonette and twelve per cent of the illegitimate children were living in rooms.

The proportion of motherless children who were occupying a whole house at eleven (86 per cent) was closer to that found among children with both parents. No significant differences appeared between the motherless children whose mothers had died and those whose parents were divorced or separated, although flat-dwelling was rather more common among the latter group.

---

1   As before, in the case of motherless children, analyses taking account of social class were confined to those from manual homes, due to the very small number in the non-manual group.

Tenure of accommodation

Information was also obtained about the type of tenure held; whether the children's families owned or were buying their home, rented it from a local authority, or were living in privately rented accommodation, either furnished or unfurnished.

According to the 1971 General Household Survey just over half (52 per cent) of the households in England and Wales were owner occupiers, a figure which has been steadily rising and which reflects the perceived advantages of home ownership in terms of both economic security and social prestige. As far as security of tenure is concerned, however, renting from the local authority is an equally sound alternative, and may have added advantages, particularly for the fatherless family, with regard to such factors as the cost and carrying out of maintenance and repairs. It is in the privately rented sector that, in spite of recent protective legislation, tenants are likely to pay more for less security and poorer accommodation.

Since, in general, owner occupation and private tenancy represent respectively the most and least advantageous forms of tenure, it was decided to look first at the number of children in different family situations who were living in owner occupied homes, and then to compare the relative proportions in the privately rented sector.

i) Owner-occupied accommodation

Regardless of the cause of the situation, families in which the father was absent were much less likely to be owner occupiers than those in which both parents were present. Altogether only half as many fatherless as two-parent families owned their homes (25 per cent as against 50 per cent). (Table A9.2 (a)). There were also marked differences among the three fatherless groups, however, with home ownership twice as common among widows (38 per cent) as among mothers whose marriage had broken down (19 per cent), and least common of all among mothers of illegitimate children (12 per cent).

Children in motherless families were also less likely than those with both parents to be living in owner-occupied accommodation (36 per cent compared with 50 per cent). However, further analysis showed that this difference largely reflected the social class distribution in the two groups, for when those from manual backgrounds were examined separately there was no significant difference between them (Table A9.2 (b)). Comparing the motherless children with their fatherless counterparts showed that the former were more likely to be living in owned homes and, in contrast to the fatherless, did not differ in this respect according to the reason for the family breakdown.

To what extent was the loss of the father associated with the loss of owner-occupied accommodation? It was possible to provide some assessment of this by looking at the tenure situation in three different family situations when the children were eleven:

Group 1 Both own parents at seven and eleven;

Group 2 Both own parents at seven, fatherless at eleven (father dead);

Group 3 Both own parents at seven, fatherless at eleven (marital breakdown).

Each group included only those whose families had been owner occupiers at the first follow-up stage, when the children were seven years old. Among families in which both parents were present throughout and among those in which the father had died, 95 per cent of those who had owned their homes when the children were seven were still owner occupiers four years later (Table S9.3). Where families had become fatherless as a result of marital breakdown, however, the figure was only 67 per cent. It was not possible from the information available to establish whether the marital breakdown preceded or followed the move from owner-occupied accommodation. The present findings could imply that divorce and separation carry a relatively high risk that mother and children will lose an owned home, while it might also be the case that the loss of such accommodation produces, or adds to, a stressful situation which culminates in marital breakdown.

ii) *Privately rented accommodation*

Several studies have drawn attention to the disproportionate number of fatherless families living in privately rented accommodation. The actual estimates vary according to the nature of the samples studied: in the Department of Health and Social Security report on 'Families Receiving Supplementary Benefit' (1972) the figure was one in four; Marsden (1969) reported that one in three of his unsupported mothers on National Assistance were in privately rented housing, while Holman (1970) found as many as 47 per cent among a group of (mostly) unmarried mothers.

The findings from the present study show that altogether 17 per cent of the fatherless children were living in privately rented accommodation at eleven, compared with only seven per cent of those in two-parent families (Table A9.2 (a)). Again, however, the cause of the father's absence was an important factor, for there was little difference between widows' children and those in two-parent families. It was among the families broken by divorce or separation, or where the study child was illegitimate that the high proportions in privately rented housing were concentrated (20 per cent and 26 per cent respectively).

Among the motherless children the number living in the privately rented sector (11 per cent) was only slightly higher than the figure for children in two-parent families; nor was there any significant difference among the motherless themselves when the cause of the situation was taken into account.

It seems likely that, with the exception of widows, a substantial proportion of fatherless families are obliged to turn to the privately rented sector for accommodation as a direct result of their family circumstances. The income restrictions associated with the loss or absence of the father mean that such families are unlikely to be able either to obtain or to maintain a mortgage, (the Supplementary Benefit system allows for repayment of mortgage *interest*, but not of capital); while the regulations governing eligibility and priority for local authority housing may in practice work to the detriment of the family without a father (Catholic Housing Aid Society, 1972; Finer Report, 1974)

The fatherless family forced into the privately rented sector, especially into furnished accommodation, is in a particularly vulnerable position, and there is ample documentary evidence to illustrate the plight of such families (Blake, 1972; Catholic Housing Aid Society, 1972). The least fortunate may find themselves trapped in a downward spiral with regard to accommodation, with little hope of escape from a depressing and threatening world of high rents, inadequate facilities, overcrowding and poor, sometimes even dangerous, physical surroundings.

Data from our own study provided an opportunity to make some quantitative comparisons between the housing standards of fatherless and two-parent children[1] living in privately rented homes. The results of these comparisons will be described in the following sections, which look at further aspects of the housing situation of the children in the study.

Availability of basic amenities

We have already shown that, depending on the cause of their family circumstances, fatherless children were less likely than those living with both parents to enjoy the benefits of living in a whole house, or in a home that was owned, and more likely to be living in privately rented accommodation. What about the *quality* of the accommodation of the children in different family situations? During the interview with the health visitor, parents were asked whether the household had sole, shared or no use of certain basic amenities, including a hot water supply, fixed bath and an indoor toilet. Their responses showed that

---

1   The number of motherless children living in privately rented accommodation (10) was too small to be studied separately.

children in fatherless homes were less likely to have sole use of all three amenities than were those in two-parent families (75 per cent as against 87 per cent (Table A9.4). These findings reflect those of other studies in the same sphere: *'Circumstances of Families'* (1967) reported that only 73 per cent of fatherless families had sole use of all three amenities — the lowest figure for any family group studied. Marsden (1969) found that 36 per cent of his fatherless sample lacked at least one standard amenity, while Holman (1970) showed that there was no amenity of which more than half of his group of unsupported mothers had sole use. The Catholic Housing Aid Society (1972), reporting on a group of fatherless families with particularly acute housing problems found that 73 per cent of 641 mothers who approached the society for help were sharing *all* basic amenities, which included cooking facilities, bathroom and indoor toilet.

As with the previous factors investigated, the overall difference between the fatherless and two-parent families was due to the disadvantaged position of families broken by divorce or separation (where only seven out of ten had sole use of all amenities) and those with illegitimate children (where the proportion was even lower). Children whose fathers had died appeared to be no worse off in this respect than those living with both parents.

There was again no overall difference between motherless children and those in two-parent families. Children whose mothers had died tended to be less well provided for than those whose parents were divorced or separated (73 per cent and 88 per cent respectively had sole use of all amenities), but the difference was not statistically significant.

A longitudinal analysis was also carried out to see whether the loss of the father between the age of seven and eleven was related in any way to *changes* in the quality of accommodation as measured by availability of amenities. This produced similar findings to the study of change of tenure: whereas 96 per cent of families with both parents present at seven and eleven retained sole use of all amenities, as did 94 per cent of those in which the father had died, among the families which became fatherless through marital breakdown, only three-quarters of those who had sole use of all amenities at the age of seven were in the same position four years later (Table S9.5). Thus, children who remained with their mother following divorce or separation were likely to have suffered a deterioration in the quality of their accommodation as well as a change to a less favourable form of tenure, although, as pointed out earlier, it was not possible to ascertain whether the accommodation changes followed or preceded the formal break in the family.

i) Availability of amenities in privately rented accommodation

As mentioned earlier, there is ample evidence that tenants of privately rented accommodation are less well provided for in terms of housing standards than owner occupiers or council tenants, and that fatherless families are a particularly vulnerable group within the private sector. It was decided, therefore, to look at the amenities available to children in different types of family situation who were living in privately rented homes at the age of eleven. This showed that, even *within* this relatively disadvantaged area, children in fatherless families were experiencing poorer quality accommodation, with only one in three having sole use of all basic amenities compared with half of those in two-parent families — in itself of course, a disturbingly low figure (Table S9.6). Again, however, children of widows did not differ to a significant degree from those with both parents; the most disadvantaged group were the illegitimate children of whom only two out of 13 had sole use of all amenities.

ii) Availability of amenities in local authority accommodation

It has also been suggested in some reports (Department of Health and Social Security, 1972; George and Wilding, 1972; Marsden, 1969) that one-parent families may be discriminated against by some local authorities when being allocated council accommodation, and disproportionately represented in older, inferior quality housing. It was possible to investigate this claim to some extent by looking at the availability of amenities among children in different family situations living in local authority housing. This showed that fewer fatherless than two-parent families had sole use of all facilities (85 per cent compared with 90 per cent) (Table S9.7), but once again this overall difference reflected the disadvantaged situation of families which were fatherless due to divorce, separation or illegitimacy. The findings also showed that motherless families in local authority housing did not differ from two-parent families with regard to access to basic amenities (92 per cent had sole use of all facilities).

There would thus seem to be some support for the claim that mothers on their own with children tend to be found in inferior standard council accommodation, although once again it should be pointed out that some of the divorced or separated mothers may have been occupying the accommodation concerned *before* the family breakdown occurred. The findings do suggest, however, that even within the relatively secure domain of local authority housing, children in some fatherless families are disadvantaged in terms of the quality of the home in which they live.

Overcrowding

An overcrowded home with inadequate space and privacy is a poor environment in which to grow up. The frustration felt by a child with nowhere to go to be quiet and nowhere to go to be noisy will, of course, be transmitted to other members of the household suffering from similar restrictions; a situation which is likely to produce a spiralling of stresses and tensions.

The National Child Development Study employed the definition of crowding adopted by the Registrar General in the 1961 Census; that is to say, a household was considered overcrowded if there were more than one and a half persons to a room (a kitchen was counted as a room if meals were regularly taken there). This definition is open to criticism as being both too simple and too lenient, since it takes no account of the age, sex and relationship of members of the household, factors which clearly affect the use which can be made of available accommodation. For example, a family consisting of father, mother, three daughters and one son would not be classified as crowded if they occupied a flat with three rooms and a kitchen in which they ate!

The weakness of the definition is particularly striking when the position of the one-parent family is considered, for the absence of a parent will automatically lower the persons/rooms ratio without reducing the accommodation *needs* of the family. A mother, father and two children living in a two room flat and *not* eating in the kitchen would be considered overcrowded. The absence of the father would reduce the persons/rooms ratio to one and a half so that the family would no longer be defined as overcrowded. It would seem absurd to suggest, however, that the disposal of the accommodation would be altered by the change, in a way which would greatly alleviate the inconvenience caused by such cramped conditions.

With these reservations in mind, an examination was made of the level of overcrowding among the different family groups in the study. This showed that, although by definition lacking one family member, fatherless children were no less crowded than those living in two-parent families (ten per cent and 12 per cent respectively were crowded) (Table S9.8 (a)). Among those from non-manual backgrounds, the number of fatherless children who were overcrowded was too small for comparisons to be made. At the manual level, however, fatherless children, particularly those whose fathers had died *were* less likely to be crowded than their counterparts in two-parent families, (Table S9.8 (b)).

These findings are in stark contrast to those of other investigations which have studied overcrowding in fatherless families. In the Ministry of Social Security report 'Circumstances of Families' (1967) the level among the fatherless was 31 per cent while Marsden (1969) found that half of his mothers living on National Assistance had overcrowded homes. It is interesting to note that both of these studies employed a more sophisticated definition of crowding based on a bedroom index, while the Department of Health and Social Security report 'Families Receiving Supplementary Benefit' (1972), using the same definition as the present study, found an overall overcrowding rate of about seven per cent among fatherless families, a similar figure to that reported here. It would seem, then, that the definition used in the present study may well underestimate the 'true' level of crowding among fatherless children, and that as well as suffering from lack of amenities, a substantial number may also be living in cramped conditions.

A rather lower proportion of motherless children lived in crowded homes (six per cent) than was the case among children in unbroken homes (12 per cent), but the numbers involved in the motherless group were small and the difference was not statistically significant. Again however, these findings contrast with those of George and Wilding (1972) who, employing a bedroom index to assess overcrowding, found that 27 per cent of motherless families were crowded compared with 12 per cent overall in England and Wales.

i) Overcrowding in privately rented accommodation

With the exception of those whose father had died, a much higher level of overcrowding was found among all children living in privately rented accommodation, although the figure for the fatherless as a whole (17 per cent) was similar to that for two-parent children (18 per cent) and came nowhere near the three out of four reported by Marsden (1969) among his unsupported mothers in the private sector. Although the number of illegitimate children involved was very small, it was this group which appeared to be particularly disadvantaged in this area, with six out of 13 living in overcrowded conditions (Table S9.9).

Bed-sharing

The actual number of rooms available to a household indicates only the amount of space at its disposal; it reveals nothing about the ability of the family to furnish and make comfortable use of the accommodation. It was decided therefore, to employ a further measure of the quality of the children's home environment, namely, the number of children in different family situations who were sharing a bed at the age of eleven.

Perhaps the most striking finding to emerge from this analysis was the large number of children in *all* types of family who were sharing their beds. However, the proportion was much higher among the fatherless (26 per cent) than among children in two-parent families (17 per cent) (Table S9.10). The highest proportion of all (29 per cent) was found among children whose mothers were divorced or separated, a pattern which remained when social class background was taken into account. Bed-sharing was also rather more common among children in motherless families (24 per cent) than among those in two-parent homes (17 per cent), but the difference was not statistically significant. Nor was the cause of the motherless situation significantly related to the level of bed-sharing among these children, although it was more frequently found among families in which the mother died (29 per cent).

i) Bed-sharing in privately rented accommodation

Fatherless children living in privately rented accommodation were particularly likely to be sharing their beds (36 per cent altogether), reflecting especially high figures among the illegitimate (six out of 13) and those whose mothers were divorced or separated (40 per cent) (Table S9.11). Widows' children and those from two-parent families did not differ from each other and the figures for these groups (16 per cent and 17 per cent respectively) were no higher than the rates for all types of housing.

Thus, although fatherless children appeared on the whole to be no more prone to overcrowding than those living with both parents, it is clear from this analysis that in other important respects their homes were less adequate. It is obviously undesirable that children of eleven should be obliged to share their beds; the disturbed sleep and lack of privacy which such a situation implies could well exert a harmful effect on more than one aspect of development.

Number of moves of home

There is little or no evidence concerning the effects, if any, of changes of home on a child's development. It would seem reasonable to suppose that while a move would to some extent disrupt and alter a family's pattern of daily life, under normal circumstances the effects would be temporary and satisfactory adjustment soon achieved. However, when such moves are many and frequent, particularly when they are due to the force of adverse circumstances rather than to positive choice, it seems likely that any detrimental effects would be exacerbated, and the risk increased that the sense of security and stability so essential to the young child might be seriously undermined.

Information was obtained during the parental interview about the number of times the family had moved home since the study child's birth. This measure has certain limitations for the purposes of this inquiry: the long time period involved (11 years) presented a risk of error of recall, and, except in the case of illegitimate children, no distinction could be made between moves which preceded or followed the family breakdown.

With these qualifications in mind, an examination was made of the number of times each child's family had moved since his or her birth. Fatherless families were found to differ markedly from those with both parents present, but in different ways according to the reason for the father's absence. Children whose father had died had made fewer moves than almost any other group — well over a third had never moved at all, compared with only a quarter of those living with both parents (Table A9.12).

This relatively high level of stability among widows' families may in fact represent an element of disadvantage in terms of housing. Whereas the mobility of two-parent families could reflect their ability to fulfil aspirations for better housing or to adapt to the changing needs of a growing family, it may be the case that the limited financial resources of widows obliged them to remain in the same accommodation, even when, for various reasons, they may have wished to move.

On the other hand, fatherless children whose parents were divorced or separated contained by far the *lowest* proportion who had never moved — only 14 per cent. (No doubt a certain number of these children would have moved at the time of the family breakdown — Marsden (1969) found that one-third of his divorced or separated mothers had had to find a new home when they parted from their husbands.) One-quarter of the children in this group had moved four or more times; only the illegitimate group contained a higher proportion with frequent (four or more) changes of accommodation, with as many as one in five having moved five times or more.

There was little difference in the number of moves made by children in motherless families and those with both parents, although those whose mother had died, like their fatherless counterparts, were less likely to have made frequent moves, and showed the highest proportion of any family situation (39 per cent) who had never moved at all.

i) Number of moves made by children living in privately rented accommodation

The well-known problems facing fatherless families in the privately rented sector, in terms of insecurity of tenure and poor standards of accommodation, would lead one to expect that the level of mobility among such families would be relatively high. It was interesting to find then, that as far as two-parent families and those of widows, were concerned, there was little difference in the number of moves made by those in the privately rented sector and the level of mobility in all types of housing (Table S9.13). For children who were fatherless as a result of marital breakdown, however, the story was very different: only *ten* of the 68 children concerned had never moved home and one in three had experienced five or more moves! The number of illegitimate children was too small to permit a valid comparison to be made, but the pattern appeared to be similar with four of the twelve children concerned having made five or more moves.

Number of schools attended

Whether or not some moves of home preceded the breakdown in the child's family, the above findings show that illegitimate children and those who were fatherless due to marital breakdown were likely to have changed home much more often than children in other family situations. It would seem likely that a change of accommodation would be more disruptive in its effects if accompanied by a change of school, and so it was decided to look also at the number of schools attended by children in the various family groups.[1] The findings revealed no differences in the number of schools attended by widow's children and those in two-parent homes (Table S9.14). On the other hand, children who were fatherless as a result of marital breakdown or illegitimacy were more likely to have experienced several changes of school; as many as one in ten of those whose mothers were divorced or separated had been to four or more schools over a period of six years or so.

Motherless children were also found to have attended more schools than children in two-parent families, although this was chiefly due to the more frequent changes made by children whose families were broken by divorce or separation. One in eight of these children had been to four or more schools. This finding is at first surprising, since this group had not been found to move home any more frequently than children in two-parent families. It would seem likely, however, that the *reasons* behind a move of home and the location of the old and new accommodation may have differed between these families and those with both parents present. Two-parent families would be more likely perhaps to be able to plan a move so that their children's schooling would not be disrupted (e.g. by moving within the same area); whereas the motherless family which moves home may do so in response to family-orientated problems. For example, the need to be closer to relatives or other sources of support and assistance may render them less able to allow their children's educational needs to play as great a part in the decision to move.

The same reasoning, of course, applies to the fatherless children who were found to have made frequent moves of home and several changes of school. The fatherless family is more likely to be *forced* to find new accommodation as a result of economic pressure, the need to be nearer

---

1   The numbers of children attending one or two schools were combined, since in many cases, the transition from infant to junior school itself involves a change of school which could not be related to moving home or to a child's circumstances.

to relatives, friends or other sources of support, and perhaps also the obligation to follow the limited employment opportunities open to mothers on their own.

Whatever the reasons for the changes recorded here, it is clear that some children had experienced several such disruptions during the six years or so since starting school. It seems likely that the problems of adapting to a new school environment, with different curricula, teachers, teaching methods and organizational practices, together with the challenge of making new friends, is a potentially disturbing experience for a young child; and repeated upheavals of this nature might well be found to have an adverse effect on one or other aspects of their development.

Feelings about accommodation

Up to this point we have been examining relatively objective measures of the housing situation of the children in the sample. However, the way a family feels about its home, what are seen as its advantages and disadvantages, will play a part in boosting or depressing the morale of all members of a household. One of the questions put to the parent during the health visitor's interview was: 'How satisfied are you with the house (flat, etc.) you are living in?' Obviously the response to such a question will depend upon the circumstances, previous experience and current expectations of the persons concerned, yet it was felt important to discover whether the poorer housing conditions already found among certain of the fatherless families in the sample were also reflected in a lower level of satisfaction among these families.

In fact, the feelings about their accommodation expressed by parents in different family situations closely followed the variations in objective housing standards among them which the foregoing pages have described. While there was no difference in the level of satisfaction expressed by parents in two parent families and fathers caring for children on their own, mothers on their own, especially where the cause was marital breakdown or the study child's illegitimacy, were much less likely to be content with their accommodation; with one in four in each group expressing some degree of dissatisfaction (Table S9.15).

i) Feelings about privately rented accommodation

The previous findings have shown that tenants of privately rented accommodation were relatively disadvantaged in terms of the standard of housing in which they were living. It would be surprising therefore if they were not on the whole a good deal less satisfied with their accommodation than families who owned their homes or rented them from the local authority, and this was, in fact, found to be the case. In all types of family there was a relatively high proportion who expressed dissatisfaction, but this was particularly marked among fatherless families broken by divorce or separation (42 per cent) and among the very small group whose children were illegitimate (nine out of the 12 cases) (Table S9.16). Here again, it would seem that, at least in terms of *sensed* deprivation, these fatherless families are likely to be at the bottom of the pile, even when looked at in the context of a relatively disadvantaged group.

Summary and conclusions

This chapter has described the results of comparisons between children living in different family circumstances in terms of various measures of housing: the type of accommodation occupied, the tenure held, availability of amenities, level of overcrowding and bedsharing, the number of changes of home and school, and the parents' feelings of satisfaction (or otherwise) with their homes.

With the exception of overcrowding (the measure of which was somewhat unsatisfactory for the present study), fatherless families were found to be worse off in every aspect of housing studied. However, the reason for the fatherless situation proved to be a crucial factor, for apart from a rather lower level of owner-occupation, widows and their children did not appear to be at a disadvantage with regard to their housing conditions when compared with families in which both parents were present. It was among the children who were illegitimate, and those who had lost their father as a result of marital breakdown that the adverse housing conditions were concentrated. Many of the mothers of these families, faced with the problems of paying for accommodation out of drastically reduced resources, and often of actually finding new accommodation, appeared to have been forced by their family circumstances into the privately rented sector, where the competition for a shrinking proportion of the housing market, and their unattractiveness as potential tenants, is likely to oblige them to pay inflated rents for the poorest type of accommodation. The present study of the use of amenities, level of overcrowding and bedsharing and mobility among fatherless families in the privately rented sector confirms others' findings that it is in this area that the most stressful conditions and acute housing problems are to be found.

For each aspect of housing studied, the findings for children from non-manual and manual homes were examined separately and this revealed, as have other studies (e.g. Circumstances of Families, 1967), that the problems facing fatherless families were by no means confined to those in the lower half of the social scale. Among the divorced and separated mothers, the poorer standards of accommodation were just as marked − sometimes even more so − among those from non-manual backgrounds. In view of the established social class differences in housing standards, it might be hypothesized that the family breakdown would have entailed a particularly dramatic deterioration in the accommodation of these families.

As far as the motherless children were concerned, the findings reflect those of George and Wilding (1972) showing that their families tended to occupy a mid-point between two-parent and fatherless families in terms of their housing conditions. In no case, however, did they differ significantly from families with both parents present, and it appeared that the mother's absence did not result in any marked disadvantage as far as housing was concerned.

The way in which our sample of one-parent families was defined (see p. 29) precluded any study of children who became homeless, directly or indirectly, as a result of the loss or absence of one parent, or whose families were consequently broken up altogether, yet this is a grave threat which could face many such families. Packman (1968) has suggested that adverse housing conditions substantially increase the risk of a child being taken into care. Wynn (1964) quoting figures for families received into temporary (Part III) accommodation in London 1959-61, concluded that the absence of the father in a family increased the risk of homelessness by a factor of about three. The Greve Report's (1971) study of people living in temporary accommodation in London showed that over a third were incomplete families in which the mother was alone with her children.

Thus, disturbing though the findings presented here may be, they could well underestimate the gravity of the housing problems faced by mothers on their own with children, by focusing attention only on those who have managed to remain as a family unit in a home of their own.

It is not difficult to imagine the generally depressing and demoralizing effects of substandard housing conditions upon those who experience them. However, there is research evidence available which points to more specific ways in which such surroundings influence children's development. Douglas (1964) found that within each social class group, children in 'satisfactory'[1] housing scored better on a series of ability and attainment tests than children in 'unsatisfactory' homes. Davie, Butler and Goldstein (1972) have shown how overcrowding and lack of basic amenities were related to inferior performance in reading and arithmetic and poorer social adjustment when the children in the National Child Development Study sample were seven, while a later study of the same children at the age of 11 (Fogelman, 1975) found an

---

1 'Satisfactory' homes were those with not more than one adverse rating on crowding, bed-sharing and lack of amenities; 'unsatisfactory' homes had two or more ratings.

association between housing conditions and school attainment, adjust-ment *and* height. Without implying a direct, casual relationship it seems probable that living in cramped conditions and having to share or do without one or more of the most basic essentials would produce feelings of frustration and depression in all the members of such a disadvantaged household and constitute a detrimental environment in which to live and grow up. As the Greve Report (1971) pointed out: 'Exposure for any length of time to bad housing conditions, where congestion and overcrowding are a feature of life, can reduce the capacity of a mother to cope with children, housework and the many other practical and emotional demands of daily life'. It might also be hypothesized that such undermining effects of poor housing would be even more severely felt when a mother has to cope alone, in the context of the material hardship and emotional stress suffered by families without a father.

Chapter ten

Contact with the social services

We have seen in the last few chapters that the absence of a parent, particularly the father, places a family in a vulnerable position with regard to its standard of living. Not only is the income of such families likely to be drastically reduced, but many of them will be living in poorer quality and less secure accommodation than families with both parents present. Moreover, the difficulties of integrating the two full-time roles of earning a living and caring for young children is likely to restrict the employment opportunities open to lone parents of either sex, thus exacerbating the material disadvantages of such families.

Problems such as these would doubtless place strain on the most united, well-adjusted family. When they are encountered in a context of emotional tension and distress following the loss of a father or mother, it is clear that the remaining members of the family are particularly likely to need help and support, be it the informal aid of relatives, friends and neighbours or the more formal assistance which our system of social services is designed to provide. Without support from some quarter, the lone parent may sooner or later be physically or emotionally unable to cope with all the demands of his or her situation, and the family may become increasingly vulnerable to another, perhaps even more damaging experience: the need for the children to be separated from their remaining parent and received into care.

In this chapter we shall look firstly at the degree of contact which had taken place between the various social services and the different groups of families in our sample. After that, an examination will be made of the number of children in each family situation who had been received into care at some time during their first eleven years.

Family situation and contact with services

During their interview with parents, health visitors were asked to inquire whether any member of the family concerned had had contact with a social worker and/or welfare organization, either statutory or voluntary, since the study child's seventh birthday (i.e. between 1965 and 1969). This was an open-ended question and thus of uncertain reliability; the respondent may have failed to mention certain contacts which he or she considered inapplicable, or there may have been some reluctance to divulge information concerning sensitive problems such as criminal behaviour, mental health, financial troubles and so on. In addition, the relatively long time period involved (four years) may have resulted in a certain amount of error of recall.

In spite of these reservations, however, it was felt worthwhile to see if there were any variations in the actual level of contact with the various services reported by the different families in our sample. The information obtained enabled a broad classification to be made of the type of problems which had generated the contact with a particular service. These were then grouped into six categories, including the then separate Children's Department, Health, Mental Health and Education Departments, statutory and voluntary organizations concerned with material aid, and lastly, agencies involved with various aspects of criminal behaviour (although this last category also included a small number of contacts with the probation service regarding cases of adoption, or marital and other non-criminal problems).

First of all, a comparison was made of the total number of contacts with services mentioned by the parents in each family situation. This revealed a marked difference between one and two-parent families. Altogether about one in three of both the fatherless (35 per cent) and motherless (31 per cent) families had been involved with at least one service compared with only eight per cent of families in which both parents were present (table A10.1). There were also variations *within* the one-parent group however; families which had lost a parent through death were less likely to have been in touch with any social or welfare agency than those in which the situation was due to marital breakdown or illegitimacy. Among the fatherless, 22 per cent of the bereaved families had had some contact, compared with 36 per cent of those with illegitimate children, and 43 per cent of the divorced and separated, while the figures for the motherless families were again 43 per cent for families broken by divorce or separation and only 19 per cent among those in which the mother had died.

Next, an examination was made of the actual types of service with which the different groups of families had come into contact. The following figures refer to the total number of children whose families had been in touch with the service concerned and not the total number of *contacts*, which was slightly greater, since a few families had been involved with more than one branch of the department concerned.

The findings showed that, overall, fatherless families had a higher level of contact than two parent families with each of the services included (table S10.2). The only exception to this was the case of widows, whose families did not differ from those in which both parents were present with regard to contact with the Children's, Health and Mental Health departments. Widow's families, in fact, were rather *less* likely than the other fatherless families to have been in touch with any particular service or agency.

As far as the motherless families were concerned, the numbers having had dealings with each individual department were very small, especially when the group was subdivided according to the cause of the family breakdown. However, the overall figures suggested that, with the exception of the Mental Health Department, these families also had a higher level of involvement than the two parent families with each of the departments or agencies concerned.

Among the fatherless families, it appeared that the most frequently contacted services were those offering material aid. (Fourteen per cent claimed to have been in touch with such agencies compared with eight per cent of motherless families and only two per cent of those with both parents). However, since this category included the then Ministry of Social Security it is clear that the level of contact suggested by these figures is a gross underestimate, since we saw in Chapter Seven that no fewer than 47 per cent of fatherless families had received Supplementary Benefit in the twelve months prior to the interview. It seems probable that many respondents may not have regarded this particular aspect of assistance as applicable to the question put to them.

The proportion of fatherless families who mentioned contacts with the Education Department was also 14 per cent, compared with nine per cent of motherless and three per cent of two-parent families. A study of the nature of the contacts with this department revealed that, among all types of family, but especially those in which the father was absent, the great majority concerned some aspect of welfare, including applications for free school meals and grants for clothing and uniforms.

One in twelve (eight per cent) of the fatherless families had had some dealings with the Children's Department, compared with only one per cent of families with both parents present. Motherless families were the most likely of all to have been in touch with the Children's Department (11 per cent) and all cases except one involved families broken by divorce or separation.

The proportion of fatherless (eight per cent) and motherless (seven per cent) families who had been involved with agencies concerned with crime was four times as great as that found among two parent families (two per cent). As pointed out earlier however, this category included contacts with probation departments regarding marital and other non-criminal problems, and when these were omitted the figure for one-parent, especially divorced and separated families was slightly reduced. Thus, although contacts with these agencies were found more frequently among one parent families, the difference reported here should be interpreted with great caution. First of all, no information was available as to the actual nature of the contact, the member (or members) of the family involved, or the time at which the contact took place. As the figures show, the actual proportions of fatherless and motherless families involved in such contacts were very small, and offer little evidence of a marked association between the absence of a parent and any criminal or delinquent activity on the part of the members of the family concerned. The present findings certainly present no grounds for relating parental absence and the prevalence of such behaviour among the *children* included in the present sample.

A rather lower level of contact was reported between each of the family groups in the study and the remaining two departments, health and mental health. As far as the former was concerned, three per cent of fatherless families had had dealings with at least one branch of the department compared with five per cent of motherless and just one per cent of two parent families. Given that this department included in its range of provisions a number of areas of assistance such as welfare, social services and home helps, the figures quoted above seem surprisingly, and perhaps disturbingly, low. The number of families who had been in touch with the Mental Health Department was also comparatively low; the figure for fatherless families was four per cent compared with two per cent among both the motherless and two parent families.

It is clear from the findings reported here that one-parent, particularly fatherless, families had had more contact than unbroken families with the various branches of the official social and welfare organizations. In view of the greater needs which these families are likely to experience, such a discrepancy is hardly surprising. However, perhaps the most important question in this area, and one which unfortunately cannot be answered adequately from the available information, is: what proportion of 'needy' one-parent families have been reached by the services concerned, and how far has the assistance available from them met the needs which have promoted the contact? It is perhaps relevant to point out that only a small minority of one-parent families had had contact with any particular service, and that only one in three claimed to have been touch with any service at all. Even allowing for underestimates in the contacts reported, it would seem that the official services are not wholly geared to providing assistance to the one-parent family in dealing with the kinds of problems presented by the absence of the father or mother. No information was available from our study about the families' knowledge of available services, but Hunt, *et al.*, (1973) found that 'appreciable proportions' of both one and two-parent families in their sample were 'unaware' of the existence of services of which they might at some time be in need.

Children in care

While the material and emotional hardships facing the one-parent family are likely to place severe strain on parents and children alike, it seems reasonable to suppose that, except in extreme cases, such circumstances will be less damaging than the further fragmentation of the family which would be produced by the reception of some or all of the children into care. However, in view of the difficulties facing the unsupported parent, it would not be surprising to find that, for a number of reasons, their task of caring for their children is relinquished, whether it be through inability to provide for their material well-being, to obtain adequate accommodation or to cope with the physical and emotional strains of single-handed responsibility.

It is clear from official statistics that a high proportion of children in care at any one time have one or both parents missing. Wynn (1964), quoting figures produced by the Social Survey for the Home Office, estimated that a child whose father was absent was 18 times more likely to be taken into care than one living with both parents. If the mother was missing the risk increased 48 times, while if both parents were absent the risk was about 95 times greater.

Family situation and children in care

The data available from the National Child Development Study presented a rather different view of the question of children coming into care. From the information collected when the children were eleven it was possible to compare the numbers in different family situations who had been in the care of a local authority or voluntary society at some time since their birth. Looked at in this way, the figures will underestimate the total numbers who had *ever* been in care since they include only those who, at the time of the follow-up survey, were once again living with one or both parents.[1] Thus, children currently in care at the time of the survey were excluded from the analysis.

The figures available however, showed a marked difference between children in the various family situations. Of the children living with both parents, only one in 50 had been in care, compared with one in 10 of those in fatherless families and one in eight of the children whose

---

1   At the time of the follow-up, 35 children were in local authority or voluntary society residential care, and a further 32 were living with foster parents.

mother was absent (Table A10.3). Most of the children concerned had been taken into the care of a local authority, although a number of cases had been dealt with by voluntary societies.

The numbers of children in the two motherless groups who had been in care were too small for comparisons to be made between them, but among the fatherless there were differences according to the reason for the father's absence. Children of widowed mothers were only slightly more likely than those with both parents to have spent a period in care (four per cent compared with two per cent) and the difference was not statistically significant. Children of divorced and separated mothers, however, were three times as likely as those of widows to have been in care (12 per cent), while illegitimate children contained the highest proportion of all (24 per cent).

It is perhaps worth pointing out here that the time covered by the question included the whole eleven years of the child's life from birth to the follow-up survey, so that, except for the illegitimate children who had been in fatherless families since birth, some of the periods spent in care may have actually preceded the family breakdown (although it seems quite probable that, especially in cases of divorce and separation, they were in fact associated with the family's problems). The findings do suggest, however, that although the illegitimate had been 'exposed' to the risk of coming into care *as one-parent children* for longer than the other fatherless and motherless groups, it was they who appeared to be especially vulnerable in this respect as a result of their family circumstances.

No information was available concerning the immediate reason for the children being received into care, how long they remained there, or whether this distressing situation had occurred more than once. However, in view of the fact that, at the time of the follow-up survey, the children in the present study were re-united with their families, it may be that, in some cases at least, reception into care was the result of a relatively short-term crisis situation, such as the illness or hospitalization of a parent. As our follow-up study (Ferri and Robinson, 1976) illustrated, the fragile equilibrium of the one-parent family's day to day organization can be quickly shattered by an emergency of this kind, so that such families are likely to be in particular need of support from outside agencies.

Summary and conclusions

According to information received from the parents concerned, one-parent families were more likely than those with both mother and father present to have had some kind of contact with the official social services during the four years preceding the 1969 follow-up study. However, only about one in three of all one-parent families claimed to have been in touch with any organization or agency, and, in view of the range and degree of the problems facing such families, this figure might be regarded as surprisingly — and perhaps disturbingly — low. The follow-up study (Ferri and Robinson, 1976) has provided further evidence that the official social services appear ill-equipped to assist in many of the problems facing the family which loses a parent. The Finer Report (1974) also concluded that while 'not all of these problems are amenable to help from organized services . . . we believe that the personal social and educational services could play a more significant role than they do now in the lives of one-parent families.' Children living in one-parent families at the age of eleven were considerably more likely than those in two-parent homes to have spent a period in care at some time during their lives. Illegitimate children were particularly likely to have had this experience — almost one in every four of this group had been in care at some time. However, the fact that all of the children concerned were currently re-united with their families suggests that the figures quoted here underestimate the extent to which family breakdown carries a risk of being received into care, for they exclude all those currently in care and for whom the loss of the father or mother, and the resultant one parent situation, may have finally led to long-term, or even permanent, separation from the remaining members of their family.

Chapter Eleven

Parental interest and involvement

Numerous studies in recent years have drawn attention to the part played in children's development by their parents' attitudes and aspirations, in addition to more tangible factors in the home background such as social class, family size and housing conditions (Central Advisory Council for Education, 1967; Davie, Butler and Goldstein, 1972; Pringle, Butler and Davie, 1966). The National Survey of Health and Development (Douglas, 1964; Douglas, Ross and Simpson, 1968) showed that, after allowing for other relevant factors, children whose parents took a keen interest in their educational progress and had high aspirations for their future, not only achieved higher test scores and more grammar school places than expected, but were also likely to stay on at school longer, to have a better attendance record and to be seen by their teachers as hard-working. This does not, of course, imply a straightforward causal relationship; parents' attitudes will themselves be influenced by other factors — including their children's school performance, so that those whose children do well will no doubt be encouraged to hope for further successes in the future.

In spite of the wealth of research evidence concerning parental attitudes, it is rare to find this important area included in studies of the one-parent family. Kriesberg (1970) in the United States found that mothers on their own were just as concerned about their children's school grades as were mothers in unbroken families, but were less likely to hope that their children would continue their education beyond the high-school level. Kriesberg suggested that this inconsistency was the result of the financial pressures on the fatherless families and the need for extra income from the children. The limited evidence available from studies carried out in this country would seem to support this interpretation: Marris (1958) and Marsden (1969) found that some mothers expressed apprehension that their children would succeed in the 11+ selection exam, since they could not afford the expenses which a grammar school place would entail. Instead, they looked forward to the time when their children would be old enough to leave school and begin to contribute to the family income.

No study to date has looked at the attitudes and aspirations of fathers bringing up children on their own. However, the Plowden Report (1967) drew attention to the comparatively small part played in this area by fathers in manual occupations; only 12 per cent had ever visited their children's school and two out of every five had left the choice of secondary school for their children entirely to their wives. It might be hypothesized then, that for such families at least, the absence of the mother would result in a particularly low level of parental involvement in the children's education and progress.

When the children in the present sample were aged eleven, information was obtained from two sources about the attitudes and aspirations shown by their parents. Firstly, teachers in the schools attended by the children were asked to state whether the mothers and/or fathers concerned had paid a visit to the school and also to assess the level of interest shown by each parent in the child's progress. Secondly, the parents themselves were asked whether or not they wanted the child to stay on at school after the minimum leaving age, and whether they hoped that he or she would subsequently undertake some kind of further education or training.

Parental discussion with school staff

Teachers were asked whether each child's parents had taken the initiative to come and discuss his or her progress with a member of the school staff at any time during the current school year. The opportunity for visiting the school would no doubt be greater in families where both the mother and the father were present, and it was decided to look at the actual level of such parent-school contact in different family situations to see if this was affected in any way by the absence of one parent. An initial analysis looked at the findings for boys and girls separately, but as the pattern according to parental situation was the same for both sexes, the following results refer to combined figures.

Altogether the parents of 59 per cent of the children in 'intact' families had been to the school attended by the child in the study (Table S11.1(a)). Almost a third (31 per cent) of the mothers had made the visit alone; for 24 per cent of the children both parents had been involved, while a mere four per cent had fathers who had visited the schools on their own. As far as the remaining children (41 per cent) in two-parent families were concerned, neither parent had been to the school.

i) Fatherless children

A very similar overall level of contact (57 per cent) between parents and schools was found among the fatherless children and no differences appeared among these families when the cause of the situation was taken into account. This would seem to indicate that the absence of the father had made little difference to the mothers' rate of school visiting. Fifty-seven per cent of widows, 52 per cent of the divorced or separated mothers and 54 per cent of those with illegitimate children had been to the schools concerned on their own. These figures are especially noteworthy in view of the relatively high rate of full-time employment among lone mothers (one in three as against one in five of those in two-parent families – see Chapter Eight). Going out to work full-time would no doubt make it harder for a mother to manage a visit to a child's school.

A separate analysis taking social class into account produced a similar pattern of findings – except in the case of divorced and separated mothers from a non-manual background. Only about half (52 per cent) of these mothers had discussed their children's progress with the teachers, compared with three out of four widowed mothers and two-thirds of the mothers in two-parent families (Table S11.1 (b)). It is not easy to account for this finding although two factors may be of importance here. Firstly, in a middle class catchment area, parent-school contacts are more likely to be highly developed in the form of Parent–Teacher Associations and other, more informal, social inter-action between teachers and parents. Secondly, as our own findings have shown, the most common pattern of parent-school interaction among non-manual families included both mother *and* father; at the manual level it was more usual to find only the mother involved. Under such circumstances the divorced or separated mother from a middle-class background may be particularly conscious of her anomalous position, and find great difficulty in maintaining the kind of contact with her children's school which we have been looking at here.

ii) Motherless children

The working father who is bringing up his children alone is also likely to face practical problems with regard to making a visit to their school as well as the difficulties involved in undertaking a role which, in many cases, would have previously been the prerogative of his wife. Predictably, therefore, a comparison between motherless and two-parent families revealed a lower level of parent-school contact in families where the mother was absent (39 per cent as against 59 per cent). This was particularly marked in families in which the mother had died – in 70 per cent of cases no school visit had been made by the parent concerned. A similar picture emerged when families from a manual background were examined separately.

It is also important to point out, however, that a comparison of the overall level of contact between parents and schools tends to hide the extent to which the lone fathers — especially those who were divorced or separated — had 'made up for' the mothers' absence through their *own* contact with the schools concerned. The total number of *fathers* in each group who had visited the schools did not differ significantly: 29 per cent among those in two-parent families, 30 per cent of widowers and 42 per cent of divorced and separated fathers. Among the two-parent families however, only four per cent of the fathers had been to the schools on their own while the corresponding figure for widowers was 30 per cent, and for divorced and separated fathers it rose to 40 per cent. These findings would seem to suggest that a substantial number of the lone fathers had taken upon themselves a role which in 'normal' family circumstances was confined to or included the mother.

Parental interest in children's progress

The next area of investigation concerned the teachers' views of the parents' interest in their children's education. Teachers were asked to indicate whether each child's mother and/or father appeared to be: 1) over-concerned about the child's progress (expecting too high a standard); 2) very interested; 3) showing some interest or 4) showing little or no interest. No differences were found in the ratings given to parents of boys and girls according to their family situation and so once again the findings for the two sexes were combined.

i) Fatherless children

Firstly, a comparison was made of the perceived level of interest of mothers in fatherless and two-parent homes. Overall, there was a striking difference in the ratings given by teachers to the two groups: only 28 per cent of the lone mothers were seen as 'very interested' as against 42 per cent of those in two-parent families, while the corresponding proportions considered to be showing little or no interest were 22 per cent and 14 per cent (Table S11.2 (a)). There were also marked differences *among* the lone mothers, however, according to the reason for the father's absence. The ratings given to widows were in fact very similar to those awarded to mothers in two-parent families; it was the divorced and separated mothers and those with illegitimate children who were regarded by the teachers as less interested in their children; — only 21 per cent and 18 per cent respectively were seen as 'very interested', while the numbers showing 'little or no interest' were 25 per cent and 28 per cent. The relatively low level of concern attributed to mothers who had experienced marital breakdown was in no way accounted for by the disproportionate number who came from a lower social class background; in fact at the non-manual level the difference was particularly marked, with 27 per cent of the divorced or separated mothers rated as showing 'little or no interest' compared with only four per cent of widows and six per cent of mothers in two-parent families (Table S11.2 (b)).

These findings are particularly striking in the light of those reported earlier, which showed that, with the exception of divorced and separated mothers from non-manual homes, there was no difference in the number of mothers in the various family situations who had taken the initiative to visit their child's school at least once. In order to investigate this apparent anomaly more closely, an examination was made of the ratings given by teachers to mothers in different family situations who *had* made a visit to the school concerned. This showed very similar ratings given to widows and those in two-parent families, with 59 per cent and 56 per cent respectively regarded as 'very interested'. The corresponding figure for divorced and separated mothers was much lower, however, (35 per cent), and by far the smallest proportion of 'very interested' mothers was found among those whose children were illegitimate (21 per cent) (Table S11.3).

It is, of course, quite arguable that the teachers adopted other criteria in assessing parental interest, criteria which were more subtle and meaningful than the relatively crude measures available to this study and which might have revealed variations in behaviour and attitudes between mothers in different situations. However, it is unlikely that the marked differences reported here could be wholly accounted for in this way, and it seems possible that the differences in the teachers' ratings described above may at least in part reflect more basic attitudes of approval and disapproval which society in general adopts towards unsupported mothers according to the reason for their family circumstances (Goode, 1964).

ii) Motherless children

Next, the perceived level of interest shown by fathers on their own was compared with that of their counterparts in two-parent families. Not surprisingly, there was a relatively high proportion of fathers about whom the teachers felt unable to express an opinion, presumably since comparatively few fathers had actually come into contact with the schools and teachers concerned. Comparing those for whom information was available showed that fathers on their own, particularly widowers, tended to be seen as less interested in their children's progress than fathers in two-parent families (Table S11.4 (a)). When social class background was taken into account however, the difference did not reach statistical significance (Table S11.4 (b)).

School leaving age

During the interview with the health visitor, parents were asked whether they would like the child in the study to stay on at school beyond the minimum leaving age (at that time fifteen years) or to leave as soon as possible.

i) Fatherless children

The main point to emerge from an analysis of the replies was that, whatever the family situation, a majority of parents hoped that their children *would* continue their schooling beyond the age of fifteen. Comparing each group of lone mothers with families in which both parents were present showed that, as far as their *sons* were concerned, there was little difference in the aspirations expressed; roughly three-quarters of the mothers in each group hoped that the boys would remain at school. The proportion was slightly lower among mothers of illegitimate boys (67 per cent) but this did not differ significantly from that among two-parent children (Table S11.5 (a)).

The mothers' aspirations for their *daughters* showed that 76 per cent of both widows and mothers in two-parent families wished them to stay on at school (Table S11.6 (a)). The proportions among the divorced or separated mothers and those whose girls were illegitimate were somewhat lower (68 per cent in each case).

A similar pattern was found when social class background was taken into account. At both the non-manual and manual levels divorced and separated mothers were slightly less likely than widows or mothers in two-parent families to express a wish for their daughters to remain at school after 15 (Tables S11.6 (b) and (c)). In neither case, however, was the difference statistically significant, and it is perhaps more relevant to stress that the majority of divorced and separated mothers did appear to hold high aspirations for their daughters' future.

ii) Motherless children

Comparing the responses of fathers on their own with those of parents in unbroken families showed that the former, especially those whose wives had died, had somewhat lower aspirations for their sons (Table S11.5 (a)). Only 56 per cent of widowers wanted their boys to remain at school after fifteen, compared with 65 per cent of divorced or separated fathers and 77 per cent of the parents in unbroken families.

There were no significant differences in the aspirations expressed for girls in motherless and two-parent families. As with their sons, however, widowers were rather less likely than parents in complete families to wish their daughters to stay on at school (65 per cent as against 76 per cent), while a relatively high proportion (83 per cent) of divorced and separated fathers hoped that they would prolong their education (Table S11.6 (a)).

These overall trends remained when social class background was taken into account, although in each case the numbers involved were very small and the differences did not reach statistical significance.

Further education or training

Parents were also asked whether or not they wanted their children to undertake some kind of further education or training after leaving school. This was, of course, a very general question: a positive reply could refer to any one of a whole range of alternatives from university education to an apprenticeship or brief course of vocational training. However, it was felt that the answers would give some indication of the level of parental aspiration with regard to their children's future qualifications and subsequent employment status, and so a comparison was made of the number of parents in each family situation who expressed a positive wish for their sons or daughters to proceed to further training after leaving school. As was the case with school leaving age, a majority of parents in every group hoped for some kind of further training for their children (the proportions ranged from 61 per cent to 85 per cent). Among the remainder most parents appeared to be undecided on the question — very few in any family situation indicated that they definitely did *not* wish their children to undertake further education.

i) Fatherless children

Comparing the aspirations expressed for fatherless and two-parent children showed that, as far as the boys were concerned, only mothers of illegitimate children contained a lower proportion who hoped for some form of further training (71 per cent compared with 83 per cent among divorced and separated mothers, 84 per cent among widows and 85 per cent in two-parent families (Table S11.7)). Mothers of illegitimate girls were also rather less likely to hope for further training for their daughters, as were divorced or separated mothers (75 per cent in each case as against 81 per cent among both widows and two-parent families (Table S11.8)). In none of the above cases, however, were the differences very large, and it is clear that mothers in all types of family situation appeared to hold high aspirations for their children's future training.

ii) Motherless children

Turning to the aspirations of fathers on their own, it appeared that those who had experienced marital breakdown held rather higher hopes for their children's further training than the fathers who had been bereaved. Eighty-four per cent of the divorced and separated fathers wanted further training for their sons compared with only 68 per cent of the widowers (Table S11.7), while as far as daughters were concerned the proportions were 83 per cent and 61 per cent respectively (Table S11.8). In each case the numbers involved were small and the differences did not reach statistical significance, but the trend which appeared would seem to be in line with those concerning other aspects of parental attitudes and involvement, which suggested a comparatively low level of aspirations and participation in educational affairs on the part of widowers.

Outings with parents

Finally, information was available from the survey which provided a rather different measure of parental involvement. During the interview parents were asked whether they accompanied the study child on walks, outings, picnics or visits 'most weeks, occasionally or never or hardly ever'.

i) Fatherless children

First of all a comparison was made between the responses of mothers on their own and those in two-parent families. This showed that, whatever the cause of the father's absence, mothers on their own took their children out less frequently (Table S11.9 (a)). Twice as many fatherless children 'never or hardly ever' had an outing with their mothers (12 per cent compared with only six per cent of those with both parents). Illegitimate children appeared to be particularly deprived in this respect — one in five were never or only rarely taken out. At the other end of the scale, only 31 per cent of the illegitimate group were taken out 'most weeks', compared with 41 per cent of children of divorced or separated mothers, 48 per cent of widows' children and 55 per cent of those with both parents.

The picture was somewhat modified, however, by taking account of the families' social class. Among those from non-manual backgrounds, there was no significant difference between mothers on their own and those in two-parent families as far as outings with their children were concerned (Table S11.9 (b)). At the manual level, however, both widows and divorced and separated mothers took their children out less often than mothers in unbroken homes (Table S11.9 (c)).

Just how frequently a mother goes out with her children is likely to depend upon several factors, one of which is the amount of time available to her. We have already seen (Chapter Eight) that mothers on their own were more likely to go out to work, and to have full-time jobs; factors which would obviously reduce the time at their disposal for taking the children out. It was particularly interesting to find then, that there was *no* apparent relationship between the mothers' employment situation (i.e. full-time, part-time or not working) and frequency of outings with the children. In fact, among the divorced and separated mothers and mothers of illegitimate children, those who were employed appeared to take their children out rather *more* often than those who were not (Table S11.10 (a) (b) and (c)).

If the employment situation of the unsupported mothers fails to account for their less frequent outings with their children, what else could explain the marked differences which were found? One obvious factor which is likely to affect the extent to which a family goes out together is its financial circumstances, and we saw in Chapter Seven that a high proportion of lone mothers were bringing up their children on very limited resources. This by itself would clearly restrict the opportunities for outings and excursions — especially those involving high travel costs and other expenses. Another important factor, however, and one which could not be directly measured in the study, is the mother's own personal resources of morale and physical energy. It might well be that the pervasive and continuing pressures on the unsupported mother would result in fatigue and depression, and little energy or enthusiasm to take part in activities with her children. Even going out for a walk may be an uninviting and burdensome prospect to a mother in this situation. The part played by the mothers' own attitudes may be of relevance in explaining the rather unexpected findings concerning working mothers. It may be the case that the tiring and time-consuming effects of full-time work are counterbalanced by heightened morale and a wider range of social contacts among mothers who go out to work, and that this in turn is reflected in their level of activities with their children.

ii) Motherless children

Information was also available concerning the extent to which fathers accompanied their children on outings, and it was perhaps rather surprising to find that overall, fathers took their children out just as frequently as mothers. A comparison of the responses of fathers on their own and those in two-parent families showed little difference, either overall or when the cause of the mothers' absence was taken into account (Table S11.11). Altogether 52 per cent of the fathers in 'complete' families took their children out 'most weeks', compared with 46 per cent of those caring for their children singlehanded.

It might well be supposed that, in 'normal' family situations, when the father accompanies his children on outings and visits, the mother is often also involved, and that such activities are undertaken by the family as a whole. The comparable level of involvement shown by the fathers on their own in the present study would thus seem to indicate a particularly high degree of participation in activities with their children in the light of their difficult circumstances and the absence of other adult company and support.

Summary and conclusions

In this chapter we have been looking at measures of parental interest in and involvement with their children, and at their aspirations for their future education and training. As far as the mothers were concerned little difference was found between widows and those in two-parent families in any of the areas investigated. Divorced and separated mothers contained a relatively low proportion who wished their daughters to remain at school after fifteen or to proceed to further training, and those from non-manual backgrounds were less likely to have visited their children's school. No other significant differences emerged between mothers in the various family situations, although those with illegitimate children also tended to have rather lower aspirations with regard to school leaving age and further training.

Although there was very little difference in the level of parent-school contact between mothers in the various family situations, there was a marked tendency for teachers to regard those who were divorced or separated or who had illegitimate children as less interested than other mothers in their children's progress. It was suggested that this might reflect the teachers' own attitudes as much as any real differences between the mothers concerned, although further investigation would be needed in this area before any firm conclusions could be drawn.

All three groups of lone mothers were found to take their children out less frequently than mothers in two-parent families, due in part perhaps to practical restraints upon their time and resources, or to their own lowered morale and incentives.

In spite of the relatively small number of lone fathers in the study there was a consistent tendency for them to display rather lower aspirations for their children than fathers in unbroken families, although this was chiefly confined to fathers who had been bereaved. Unlike lone mothers, however, fathers on their own were found to be involved just as frequently in activities with their children as were their counterparts in complete families.

It is impossible to assess from the information available to what extent the lower aspirations found among some groups of lone parents represented a 'realistic' adjustment in the light of the practical constraints associated with their family situation, or how far they reflected more general feelings of depression and pessimism brought about by their unhappy experiences.

Whatever the case may be, it seems justifiable to conclude this analysis on a more optimistic note, for the differences which did emerge were few, and were slight in magnitude. In every aspect of parental involvement and aspirations investigated, a majority of mothers and fathers in all types of family situation showed an interest in their children's current progress, and concern for their future development and success.

Chapter Twelve

Attainment and progress in school

The findings described in the previous chapters of this report have shown clearly the extent of the disadvantage suffered by children brought up by a lone parent. The standard of living attainable by such families was likely to be seriously limited by their low level of income. The accommodation problems which they faced meant that many children were growing up in poor quality housing conditions. The difficulties inherent in combining employment and child care restricted the choice open to parents in providing for the material, physical and emotional welfare of their children. All these problems contributed to the increased risk that children cared for by lone parents would be separated from their already disrupted families and spend a period in care.

But what was the effect upon the children themselves of the absence of a parent and the accompanying hardships and problems? In this and the following chapters we turn to an assessment of the ways in which the family experiences of the children in our sample had influenced various aspects of their development, beginning in this chapter with a study of their educational attainment and progress.

The analyses which will be reported here cover two broad areas:

1. The proportion of children in different family situations receiving, or considered to be in need of, special educational treatment.

2. A comparison of the scores obtained by children in different family situations on tests of reading and arithmetic at the age of eleven, and of their relative progress between the ages of seven and eleven.

Type of school attended

Information was available from the educational assessment form about the type of school currently attended by the children in the study. This showed that very few children were going to 'special' schools of some kind — only 1.4 per cent of all those living with both parents (Table S12.1). The actual number of one-parent children attending special schools was too small for meaningful comparisons to be made between them and two-parent children, but, although none of the differences were statistically significant, the figures did suggest that a rather higher proportion of the fatherless (2.5 per cent) and the motherless (2.2 per cent) went to special schools, with the highest proportion of all among the fatherless illegitimate children (5.4 per cent).

Children likely to benefit from special schooling

The teachers were also asked whether they felt that the children concerned would *benefit* from attendance at a special school of some kind. In this case, although the actual numbers involved were again small, there *were* significant differences in the replies given, according to the children's family situation. Twice as many fatherless (3.5 per cent) as two parent children (1.7 per cent) were considered by their teachers to be likely to benefit from special educational treatment (Table S12.2). There were also twice as many fatherless as two-parent children (3.1 per cent and 1.6 per cent respectively) about whom the teachers felt unable to give a definite answer, a group which possibly contained children whom the teachers regarded as 'borderline' cases. The numbers were too small to make valid comparisons between the different fatherless groups, although the proportion of illegitimate children considered likely to benefit from special schooling was rather higher than in the other two groups.

The proportion of motherless children considered likely to benefit from special schooling (7.9 per cent) was four times greater than the figure for the two-parent children (1.7 per cent), with the highest proportion of all found among children whose mothers had died (11.4 per cent).

Children receiving help because of backwardness

Teachers were also asked whether the children in the study were currently receiving help within the school because of educational backwardness. No differences were found between children in two-parent families and those living with widowed mothers (8 per cent in each case were being helped in this way) (Table S12.3). The proportion was only slightly higher among those cared for by divorced or separated mothers, (10 per cent) but markedly greater among fatherless illegitimate children (26 per cent). Motherless children, too, were more likely than their peers in two-parent homes to be receiving assistance for backwardness (14 per cent), but the difference just failed to reach statistical significance.

It would appear then that, apart from those living with widowed mothers, children in one-parent families were rather more likely than their counterparts in unbroken homes to be receiving help for educational backwardness. These figures however, concern only a minority of the children in any family situation and our chief purpose in this part of the study was to look at the *overall* attainment level of children in one and two-parent families. The results of this investigation are described in the following sections.

Attainment in reading and arithmetic

It was pointed out in Chapter Two that, although a number of studies have looked at the relationship between the absence of a parent and children's educational performance, the results have often been inconclusive or even conflicting. This seems to be due largely to the selective nature of the samples studied, or to a failure to take account of other relevant factors in the situation, thus precluding the isolation of the 'effects' of the family situation itself.

The foregoing chapters have indicated that children living in one-parent families are likely to start out at a disadvantage compared with their counterparts in 'normal' two-parent homes. Over the years numerous studies, including those from the National Child Development Study itself (Crellin, Pringle and West (1971); Davie, Butler and Goldstein (1972)), Wedge and Prosser (1973) have demonstrated the relationship between educational performance and certain factors in the child's home background. Low social class, poor housing, low income, limited parental interest and aspirations — factors such as these are demonstrably associated with relatively poor performance in school, and it is to many such disadvantages that children in one-parent families have been seen to be particularly prone.

It was clear, therefore, that any assessment of the effects of family situation on children's educational performance would have to make allowance for factors such as these. The purpose of our investigation was to see whether the absence of a father or a mother was *in itself* related to the children's performance in reading or arithmetic, or whether any differences which emerged could be accounted for by other factors which distinguished between children in different family situations.

Method of analysis

The method of investigation used was an analysis of variance. Basically, this approach enables an estimate to be made of the association between a particular factor, in this case family situation, and say, reading score, after making allowance for the 'effect'[1] of other factors known or suspected to be associated with performance in the area under investigation.

Included in the analysis was a range of factors likely to be related to attainment in reading or arithmetic and/or which had already been shown to be associated with family circumstances. In addition to the parental situation itself the analysis included the child's sex, social class background, family size, receipt of free school meals as an indicator of income level, the availability of basic household amenities, whether the child had ever been in care, number of schools attended, mother's educational level and employment situation, and parents' aspirations with regard to school leaving age.

To be included in the analysis each child had to have information available in all the above-mentioned areas. This presented a problem, not only by seriously reducing the numbers in certain groups, but because none of the illegitimate children had information on social class which was comparable to that available for all the other groups (see Chapter Six). Also, the motherless children, by definition, had no details regarding mothers' employment situation.

In order to overcome these problems two separate analyses were carried out. The first left out all the illegitimate children and thus included five family situations: children in two-parent families and those who were fatherless or motherless, subdivided according to whether the cause was bereavement or marital breakdown. Mothers' educational level and employment situation were also excluded from this analysis. The second analysis left out all motherless children but included those who were illegitimate, and also the information concerning the mothers' education and work status.

As part of the follow-up study, tests of reading comprehension and mathematics had been included in the test booklet administered to the children in school, and the scores obtained in these tests were used as measures of their attainment in each area. The reading test was of the 'sentence completion' type, while the mathematics test included, in addition to mechanical arithmetic questions, items designed to test the child's understanding of mathematical concepts.[2]

Family situation and attainment in reading
Analysis (1) (excluding illegitimate children)

Apart from the child's sex, each of the factors included in the first

---

1 The word 'effect' refers here and elsewhere in this report to the *relationship* between two variables in the context of the particular analysis described. It does *not*, therefore, imply any causal connection between the variables concerned, and is always placed in quotation marks in order to warn the reader against such misinterpretation.

2 Both tests were constructed by the National Foundation for Educational Research.

analysis was found to be significantly related to reading score when no allowance was made for any of the other factors. This remained the case when all the other factors *were* taken into account — with the one exception of family situation. The result of allowing for all other factors was to reduce the differences between children in the various family groups so that they were no longer statistically significant (Figure 1 and Table A12.4). Not only was the *size* of the differences between the groups reduced however, but their position in relation to each other was also changed. Looking at the average raw scores for each group, it appeared that children who were fatherless due to marital breakdown had the lowest scores of all, but the effect of allowing for all the other factors was to change the 'rank order' of the various groups so that this was no longer the case. It was particularly interesting to discover that when 'receipt of free school meals' was left out of the analysis, the relationship between family situation and reading score again became statistically significant, with the children who were fatherless through marital breakdown again showing the lowest scores (Table S12.5). This did not occur when any other single factor was omitted and could mean that low income and its attendant problems is a major contributing factor in the poorer overall reading performance of children in fatherless families.

This point can perhaps be made more clearly by looking at the scores in a rather different way. Whatever their parental situation, children in families receiving free meals did less well in reading than those whose families were not in this low income group (Table S12.6). However, looking only at those who *were* receiving free meals showed that children in the two fatherless groups actually obtained *higher* average scores than their counterparts from two-parent homes. The same was true when children from families *not* receiving free meals were compared. The reason for the lower *overall* score of children in fatherless families was the very high proportion in these groups who were having free meals (49 per cent of widows children and 69 per cent of those whose mothers who were divorced or separated, compared with only 8 per cent of children in families with both parents). Thus, when allowance was made for low income as measured in this way, the fatherless children 'improved' considerably in relation to those in two parent homes.

Receipt of free school meals was much less common in motherless families (17 per cent) than among those in which the father was absent, and motherless children obtained lower reading scores than those in two-parent homes regardless of whether they had free meals.

The performance of the motherless children as measured in this analysis is particularly difficult to assess. The two motherless groups showed the lowest reading scores *after* allowance had been made for all

Figure 1: Reading Score at 11: analysis of variance (1)

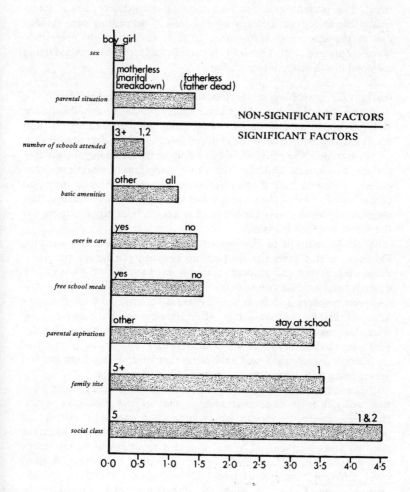

number of points of score difference (fitted constants)
(test range = 0—35)

other factors. There would thus seem to be a tendency for children in these families to do less well in reading than their peers in other family circumstances, although the numbers of motherless children were very small. The present evidence thus remains inconclusive, but it seems reasonable to suggest that any adverse 'effect' on reading performance due to the absence of the mother is likely to be of slight magnitude when compared with the 'effects' attributable to the other factors included in this analysis (see Figure 1).

Analysis (2) (excluding motherless, including illegitimate children)

As mentioned earlier, the second analysis included the illegitimate children and the two factors concerning mothers' education and employment, but excluded the children living in motherless families.

To overcome the problem of not having comparable social class data for the illegitimate children, the other three family situations (two-parent, widowed and divorced/separated) were each split into two according to whether their background was non-manual or manual. The illegitimate children were then treated as a seventh 'family situation' for the purposes of comparison.

A similar pattern of findings emerged as in the previous analysis, although in this case, the relationship between the family situation/social class factor and reading score remained significant when all the other factors were taken into account (Table A12.7). Children living with widowed mothers and from a non-manual background were found to have the highest average scores after allowing for the other factors, while the lowest scores were obtained by those from manual homes who were fatherless as a result of marital breakdown. The position of the illegitimate children was similar to that of children from manual homes living with both parents or with widowed mothers.

Since social class background was combined with family situation in this analysis it is clear that at least part of the difference which emerged between the various family groups was due to the association between reading score and social class. Within each family situation children from non-manual homes obtained significantly better scores than those from manual backgrounds. However, comparing children from different family situations but from *similar* social class backgrounds showed that, at both the non-manual and manual levels, children living with divorced or separated mothers tended to do less well than widows' children or those in two parent families. This result, combined with the fact that a similar trend was found in the previous analysis, suggests that the loss of the father through marital breakdown may itself have an adverse, although relatively slight, 'effect' on children's reading.

Mother working and reading attainment

The second analysis also included details of the mother's employment situation — whether she had worked full-time, part-time or not at all in the year preceding the survey. The findings showed that, taking the sample as a whole, there was no difference in the reading performance of children whose mothers had worked part-time and those whose mothers had not been employed, but that where mothers had had full-time jobs the children tended on the whole to read less well.[1]

However, it also emerged from the analysis that the relationship between the mothers' employment situation and the children's reading performance varied according to the family situation. It was only among the children in two-parent families that mothers' full-time working was associated with lower reading attainment. Among the illegitimate children, those whose mothers worked full-time actually scored significantly *better* in reading than those whose mothers had not worked or had only held part-time jobs (Table A12.8). There were no significant differences within the other two fatherless groups, although there was also a slight tendency for widows' children to do better if their mothers had been employed full-time.

These differences *within* the various family groups were also apparent when comparisons were made *between* them. The reading scores of illegitimate children whose mothers had worked full-time did not differ significantly from those of children in other family situations from non-manual backgrounds. They were, however, significantly *better* than those of children from *manual* backgrounds who were living with both parents or with divorced or separated mothers (Table A12.8). This is a particularly striking finding, for although they lacked comparable social class information, it was seen in Chapter Six that the majority of the illegitimate children had mothers whose *own* background had been manual, while other research (Crellin *et al.*,1971) has suggested that illegitimate children are 'downwardly mobile' on the social scale. The present results would thus seem to suggest that for these children, the mother's full-time employment was associated with a real boost in reading score, since their performance was comparable to that of children in other family situations from a more advantageous social background. In contrast, illegitimate children whose mothers had not worked or who had only had part-time jobs did less well than all other groups, (although they did not differ significantly from children in other family situations who came from manual backgrounds).

This is not, of course, to imply a direct causal relationship between

---

1 It is worth noting, however, that this difference, in spite of reaching statistical significance, was comparatively small.

mother working and reading score among these children. However it does add some support to the suggestion, put forward in Chapter Eight, that among some unsupported mothers, full-time employment may be associated with other factors which exert a favourable influence on the children's development. In view of the previous discussion of the factors likely to discourage lone mothers from taking up full-time work, it also seems likely that those who had done so were the ones able to obtain the more rewarding jobs both in financial and other respects. Directly or indirectly such factors would no doubt make a positive contribution to their material, social, and psychological resources in coping with the demands of their family situation.

One plausible suggestion, of course, is that the mothers who obtain full-time jobs are likely to be the most able and best qualified, and that these factors will be related to positive outcomes in terms of the children's development. However, our earlier findings showed that only one in seven of the mothers of illegitimate children had stayed at school beyond the statutory leaving age, so that this would seem to be an inadequate explanation for the differences in reading performance reported above.

The finding that the relationship between mother working and children's attainment varied according to the family situation is a particularly interesting one, and underlines the complexity of this situation noted by other investigators (Stolz, 1960; Wallston, 1973). However, in considering the possible implications of these results for unsupported mothers and their children, the following cautionary remarks seem particularly appropriate:

> 'Care must be taken in using conclusions about positive or detrimental effects of maternal employment on children to encourage or discourage mothers interested in working. Until causation can be shown, there is danger in drawing implications for relevant social action . . . . .'   (Wallston 1973)

Family situation and attainment in arithmetic

The two analyses employed to assess the children's reading attainment were then repeated, using scores on the arithmetic test as a measure of achievement in this area.

Analysis 1 (excluding illegitimate children)

As had been found with reading, every factor except for the child's sex was significantly related to arithmetic score when no allowance was made for the other factors. Unlike the reading test however, although taking account of all the other factors reduced the overall differences

Figure 2: Arithmetic score at 11: analysis of variance (1)

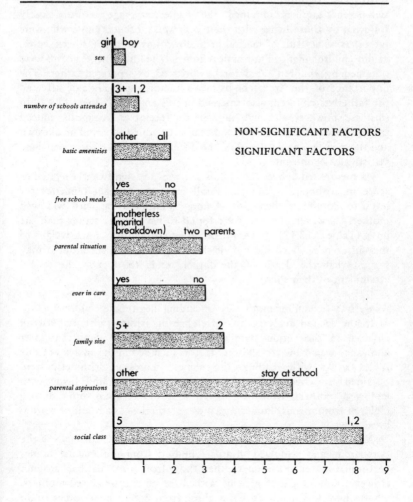

Number of points of score difference (fitted constants)

(test range = 0—40)

between children in various family situations, they still remained statistically significant (Figure 2 and Table A12.10). Children in two-parent families obtained the highest average scores, closely followed by those living with their widowed mothers. Those who were fatherless as a result of marital breakdown however, had lower scores, as did children living in motherless homes. The lowest scores of all were obtained by children cared for by divorced or separated fathers. The importance of the 'free schools meals' factor, especially as it affected the fatherless children, also emerged in this analysis (Table S12.11). In this case, however, although allowing for receipt of free meals reduced the gap between children who were fatherless due to marital breakdown and those in two-parent families, the difference between them remained statistically significant.

As mentioned above, the child's sex was not significantly related to score in arithmetic, although overall there was a slight tendency for boys to do better than girls. Among children living with widowed mothers, however, the girls were found to have higher scores than the boys (Table A12.12). It would be rash to attach too much weight to this difference, which did not reach statistical significance, but it may suggest that the death of the father tends to depress the school attainment of their sons.

Analysis 2 (excluding motherless, including illegitimate children)

In the second analysis too, differences in arithmetic score between children in the various family situations remained significant after allowance was made for all other factors included in the analysis (Table A12.13). As with reading, the highest scores in arithmetic were obtained by children from a non-manual background living with widowed mothers, while the lowest scores were again found among children from manual homes which were fatherless as a result of marital breakdown.

As with reading too, it was not surprising to find that *within* the two-parent and widowed groups, children from non-manual homes performed better in arithmetic than those from a manual background. However, among children living with divorced and separated mothers, whilst there was a tendency for those from non-manual homes to do better, the difference between them and the manual group was not statistically significant. The findings reported in Chapter Eleven suggested that children living with divorced or separated mothers in non-manual homes were somewhat disadvantaged in terms of their mothers' interest in their schooling (as perceived by teachers) and aspirations for their educational future. It seems possible that such factors may have played a part in the relatively depressed performance of these children which this analysis has revealed.

Mother working and arithmetic attainment

A study of the relationship between the mothers' employment situation and their children's performance in arithmetic revealed a similar pattern to that found in the analysis of reading, with the 'effect' of the mother working varying according to the family situation (Table A12.14). Once again, children from two-parent families whose mothers had worked full-time did less well than those whose mothers had not worked or had had part-time jobs. Among the fatherless, however, illegitimate children and those living with widowed mothers tended to do better if their mothers had had full-time jobs.

Again, interesting differences emerged when comparisons were made *between* family situations according to mothers' employment situation. The performance of the illegitimate children did not differ significantly from that of their peers in non-manual homes (whether fatherless or living with both parents) if their mothers had worked full-time. On the other hand, if their mothers had not been employed or had had part-time work, the illegitimate did less well than all the other groups, although their performance was not significantly worse than that of children in other family situations from manual backgrounds.

As far as widows' children were concerned, those whose mothers had worked full-time achieved higher scores than their counterparts from two-parent families or those living with divorced or separated mothers. This was the case at both social class levels, although among those from manual homes, the difference between the widows' and two-parent children did not reach statistical significance.

Where widowed mothers had not worked or had had only part-time jobs, there was no difference at the non-manual level between their children and those in two-parent homes, but in the manual group, the widows' children actually did *less* well than those in unbroken families.

As was the case with reading, the mothers' employment situation appeared to be less important for the arithmetic performance of children living with divorced and separated mothers than for those in other fatherless families. Whether their mothers had worked or not children who were fatherless through marital breakdown did less well in arithmetic than those in two-parent families. Both this analysis and that investigating reading performance have indicated that the mothers' full-time employment was associated with a higher level of achievement among illegitimate children and those living with widowed mothers, but that as far as children of divorced or separated mothers were concerned this was not the case. What could account for these differences between the various groups of fatherless children?

It was suggested earlier that unsupported mothers who undertake full-time work will tend to be those for whom such employment represents a financially viable proposition. Such families are likely to be somewhat better off materially than their counterparts who remain dependent upon state aid (Hunt *et al.*, 1973). In addition, the social contacts and stimulation of the employment situation may be of particular benefit to lone mothers, and these benefits are likely to be reflected in their relationships with their children and indirectly, in the children's own development. It was noted in Chapter Eight that other investigations have shown a positive association between unsupported mothers working and their aspirations for their children (Kriesberg, 1970) and also between their own employment and aspects of the children's social development (Nye, 1957). Our present findings suggest that, for illegitimate children and those cared for by widow mothers', full-time work is also positively related to school attainment.

But why should the same not apply to children of divorced or separated mothers? Two points may help to explain the discrepancy between these and other fatherless families. Firstly, for many divorced and separated mothers, the choice between working full-time and relying on state aid appears to be, in financial terms at least, one of the 'Hobson's' variety. We saw in Chapter Eight that very few had obtained professional or other high level jobs, and most of those working were in manual or other low-paid occupations. However, the same disincentives to employment apply to mothers of illegitimate children, so cannot fully explain the differences referred to above.

Perhaps a more important factor in relation to the divorced/separated group concerns the family breakdown itself. This had, no doubt, often been surrounded by tensions and distress of a long-term nature, which in many cases perhaps were still continuing. Such factors are likely to have played a major part in the generally poorer school performance of the children in these families, and may well have outweighed any variations due to the mothers' work situation.

Family situation and educational progress

We have seen in the foregoing pages that the attainment in reading and arithmetic of our eleven-year-old children differed according to their family situation. But how had this experience affected their *progress* during the time they had spent in the junior school? During the first follow-up of the children in the National Child Development Study tests of reading and arithmetic had been given to the seven-year-olds, and the result of these tests had to be taken into account in assessing progress made four years later. For example, a child who scored 35 out of 40 on the reading test at eleven had not necessarily made better *progress* than one who scored only 30, if the two started off from different levels of attainment at seven.

It was initially proposed to confine this analysis to children who were fatherless due to death or marital breakdown and to compare the progress of those who had lost their father before seven with those who became fatherless after that age, and with children who had remained with both parents throughout the period. However, the data showed no apparent difference in progress according to the time of the family breakdown. It should be remembered that the first fatherless group contained some who at seven had only just lost their father and others who had been fatherless since infancy; while in the group who became fatherless *after* the age of seven, particularly those in families subsequently broken by divorce or separation — there would doubtless be children already suffering at seven from the stresses of the coming family disruption. As a result, neither group was homogeneous with respect to family experience and it was not altogether surprising that no difference emerged between them in relation to the childrens' progress. No conclusions can thus be drawn from the present study concerning the relevance of the age at which family breakdown occurs.

It was decided therefore to re-combine the groups of fatherless children and to compare the progress of all those whose fathers had died with all children whose mothers were divorced or separated, and with the children in two-parent families. The two groups of motherless children were also included in the analysis, but not those who were fatherless due to illegitimacy. It was considered important to take full account of social class background and, as mentioned before, such information was not available for the illegitimate children.

Two analyses of variance were then carried out to measure progress in reading and arithmetic. In addition to family situation and social class, the children's sex and their score in reading and arithmetic at seven were also included.

Progress in reading between seven and eleven

The results showed that boys had made better progress than girls in reading between seven and eleven. This reflects a narrowing of the gap between the sexes — girls had performed significantly better than boys at seven, but there was no difference between them by the age of eleven. The child's social class background was also related to progress in reading — for a given level of attainment at seven children from higher social class homes were doing better by the age of eleven than their counterparts from lower social class backgrounds.

Family situation was also found to be related to reading progress, with the children in two-parent families having drawn slightly, though significantly, ahead of those who were fatherless due to marital breakdown (Table A12.15). Children in motherless families, however, and those living with widowed mothers did not differ significantly from children in two-parent homes, although there was a tendency for the motherless children, especially those in families broken by divorce or separation, to have made rather poorer progress.

Progress in arithmetic between seven and eleven

Unlike reading, the child's sex was not found to be significantly related to progress in arithmetic between seven and eleven. As with reading, however, it appeared that the higher the social class background, the better the progress made in arithmetic.

Family situation was also found to make a difference here, with children in two-parent families showing significantly better progress than those who were fatherless due to marital breakdown (Table A12.16). Children living with widowed mothers did not on the whole differ significantly from those in two-parent families, but within the former group the performance of boys and girls was rather different. Widows' daughters in fact did slightly (although not significantly) better than girls in two-parent homes, but their sons, like those who were fatherless due to marital breakdown, had made significantly *poorer* progress than boys in complete families (Table S12.17). Thus, while there was no difference in the progress made by boys and girls in two-parent families or those fatherless due to marital breakdown, among children of widowed mothers the girls had made significantly better progress in arithmetic than had the boys. This finding reflects the tendency noted in the previous analysis of attainment at eleven and confirms the suggestion put forward there that the death of the father had an adverse effect upon the performance of their sons, particularly as far as arithmetic was concerned. It seems that the presence and support of the father might be particularly important for the development of their sons' quantitative skills, especially as boys grow older.

This difference between the progress of boys and girls was not apparent, however, among children who were fatherless due to marital breakdown. In this case both boys and girls had made poorer progress than their counterparts in two-parent families. It might be hypothesized that it is only in cases of bereavement that boys' performance is depressed by father absence, but it seems more likely that the particularly disadvantageous circumstances suffered by families broken by divorce or separation outweighed any differential effects upon boys and girls which might have been due to the reason for the fathers' absence.

No significant differences emerged in the arithmetic progress of motherless children and those living with both parents although, as with reading, there was a tendency for the motherless children to have dropped behind somewhat by the age of eleven.

The findings of this longitudinal analysis have thus indicated that except for girls cared for by widowed mothers, living in a one-parent family was associated with a relative *deterioration* in reading and arithmetic performance between the ages of seven and eleven. This result should be treated with caution however, as the situation was particularly complex, due to wide differences in the time which had elapsed since the family breakdown and the relationship between the time of the breakdown and the stages at which the children were tested. Nonetheless it does appear that the adverse 'effects' associated with the loss of a parent are long-term — at least in the areas studied here. It would seem particularly important, therefore, to assess the subsequent progress of the same groups of children, in order to see whether those in one-parent families continued to deteriorate relative to children in unbroken homes, whether their position became stabilized, or whether they later managed to regain some of the ground which they had lost.

Summary and conclusions

The analyses reported in this chapter have shown that the family situation in which the children were living at the age of eleven was related to their current performance in reading and arithmetic, and to the progress they had made since the age of seven. However, the cause of the situation was also found to be of major importance.

In both areas, the attainment level of children living with widowed mothers was, on the whole, similar to that of children in two-parent families. There was thus little evidence that the death of the father had itself had an adverse effect on the children's attainment, although there was a tendency for the boys in such families to have done less well than the girls. In general however, any reaction to the shock of bereavement which might have affected their school progress appeared to have been largely overcome by the time of the follow-up survey.

The position of children who were fatherless as a result of marital breakdown however, was very different. Their performance in arithmetic was significantly poorer than that of children in two-parent families and, although the difference was less marked, our findings have suggested that they were reading less well too. The relatively poor attainment of these children was found to be strongly associated with disadvantaging factors in their background and environment, such as low income and financial hardship, poor housing, low social class and so on. However, such factors did not account for *all* of the difference in performance between these children and their peers from two-parent homes, and it did appear that their family experience itself was, directly or indirectly, related to the children's academic progress. The finding that arithmetic performance in particular was affected by the family situation of these children provides some support for the claims of other investigators that quantitative, rather than verbal, aptitudes are depressed by the absence of the father, (Funkenstein, 1963; Carlsmith,

1964; Gregory, 1965).

The assessment of illegitimate children cared for by their mothers alone was rather more complicated. In both reading and arithmetic, when all the other factors were taken into account, the performance of these children did not differ from that of children in non-manual two-parent families if their mothers worked full-time and was comparable to that of their counterparts in manual two-parent families when their mothers had not worked or had held part-time jobs. It would seem then that, although the illegitimate children appeared to be doing much less well than those in two-parent families when only their 'raw' scores were compared, the difference was attributable to handicapping factors *associated* with being illegitimate and fatherless, rather than to their birth status as such, or to the absence of a father in itself. It should be stressed, however, that our group of illegitimate children was small in number and that these findings should be regarded as tentative.

As far as the motherless children were concerned it appeared that, regardless of the cause of the situation, the absence of the mother was associated with a comparatively poor level of attainment in arithmetic, while there was also a tendency for motherless children to read less well than their counterparts in two-parent families. Again, however, the number of children in the two motherless groups was small, and the findings, particularly those concerning reading attainment should be treated with caution.

In conclusion, it should be pointed out that although their family situation was found to be related to the childrens' attainment and progress, the 'effects' attributable to the absence of a parent *per se* were relatively small when compared with those due to other factors included in the analysis, such as social class, family size, and parental aspirations.

However, the teacher in the classroom situation is likely to compare children in terms of their actual performance and cannot be expected to take account of all 'relevant factors' in the way in which our analysis has done. In terms of straightforward scores, children from one-parent families were certainly doing less well than those from unbroken homes, and it is perhaps worth drawing attention to the implications of such differences for teachers' expectations. Increasing attention has been paid in recent years to the interplay between pupils' performance in school and what their teachers expect from them. (Rosenthal and Jacobson, 1968; Pidgeon, 1970). It seems not unreasonable to suggest the awareness of family breakdown or anomalous family circumstances might have the effect of reducing teachers' expectations concerning the children from such homes; expectations which might themselves then constitute a further handicapping factor in the development of already disadvantaged children.

Chapter Thirteen

The children's behaviour and adjustment

It is widely believed that the loss or absence of a parent has an adverse effect on the emotional and social development of the children concerned, and this is perhaps the most widely investigated aspect of the effects of family breakdown. Yet, as was shown in Chapter Two, the evidence from the numerous studies which have been carried out in this area remains inconclusive. This seems to be due in part to differences in the samples studied. Some, for example, take no account of current family circumstances, others look only at a particular group of one-parent children, such as sons of widowed mothers. In addition, the wide variation in the aspects of personality and adjustment investigated, ranging from delinquency and anti-social behaviour to self-image and sex-role development, have made it difficult to compare the results of different studies.

Information collected for the National Child Development Study made it possible to study wide-ranging aspects of the behaviour and adjustment of the children in the sample. Their behaviour in school was assessed by means of the Bristol Social Adjustment Guide, which was completed for each child by teachers in the schools concerned. The parental interview schedule contained a lengthy list of questions about the child's behaviour at home. Parents were also asked whether the child in the study suffered from nocturnal enuresis, an area which has previously received attention in studies of the relationship between parental absence and emotional disturbance (Douglas, 1970). Using all this information, comparisons were made of the behaviour and adjustment of children in the different family situations in our sample.

Behaviour and adjustment in school

As mentioned above, the instrument used to assess the school behaviour of the children in the National Child Development Study sample was the Bristol Social Adjustment Guide. This contains some 250 descriptions of behaviour, and teachers are asked to underline those which 'best fit' the child in question. By means of the coding system accompanying the Guide, the summation of particular items gives a total score indicating the child's level of adjustment; the higher the score, the poorer the adjustment.

Clearly, a measure such as this lacks the objectivity of a standardized attainment test, and will to some extent reflect the attitudes and values of the teachers, and the middle-class norms of the school. The fact that children from particular social groups show a lower degree of conformity to such norms may not necessarily be an indication of maladjustment in the psychological sense. On the other hand, some of the behaviour described in the Guide would be less questionably regarded as 'deviant' or abnormal, and, while the above reservations should be borne in mind, it was felt that the Guide provided a useful measure of the school behaviour of children in different family situations.

The method adopted to compare children in one and two-parent families was the same as that used in the study of their school attainment, that is, an analysis of variance. This enabled allowance to be made for differences in the background and experience of the children concerned. As before, two separate analyses were carried out[1] in order that all the following factors could be included: family situation, sex, social class background, family size, receipt of free school meals, availability of basic household amenities, number of schools attended, parental aspirations, mother's education and employment situation and whether the child had ever been in care.

Analysis 1 (excluding illegitimate children)

This analysis, which excluded all the illegitimate children, compared the social adjustment of children in two-parent families with that of children who were fatherless or motherless as a result of death or marital breakdown.

Each of the separate factors included in the analysis was found to be significantly related to social adjustment when no account was taken of any of the other factors.[2] As far as parental situation was concerned, children who had lost either parent as a result of divorce or separation appeared less well adjusted than widows' children or those in two

---

1 The reasons for carrying out two separate analyses are described in Chapter Twelve.
2 In contrast to the results of the analysis of attainment the child's sex was found to be significantly associated with adjustment at the age of 11, with girls being seen by their teachers as better adjusted than boys (tables A13.1 and A13.2

Figure 3: Social adjustment at 11: analysis of variance (1)

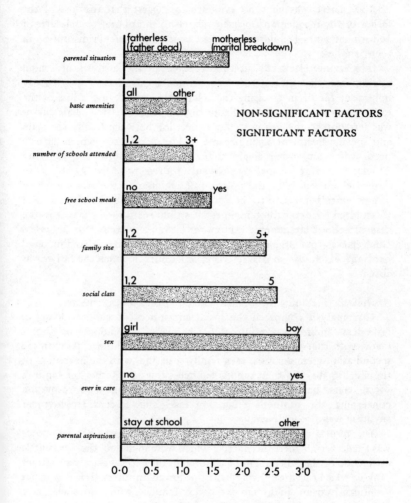

number of points of score difference
(fitted constants)

parent families. When allowance was made for the other factors however, the differences between children in the various family situations were no longer statistically significant (Figure 3 and Table A13.1). There was thus no evidence to suggest that the loss of the father or the mother was *in itself* related to the poorer overall level of adjustment among children who had experienced such a disruption in their families.

It was interesting to discover that, as in the analysis of school attainment, the receipt of free school meals was a particularly important factor in assessing the relationship between the loss of the father and the children's social adjustment. When the 'free meals' factor was left out of the analysis, the association between family situation and social adjustment again became significant, a result which did not occur when any other single factor was omitted (Tables S13.3 and S13.4). The effect of making allowance for receipt of free meals was to 'improve' considerably the position of children in the two fatherless groups, in relation both to their counterparts in motherless families and to children in two-parent families. It would seem then that, as in the case of school attainment, the poorer overall adjustment of fatherless children was to a large extent associated with the financial and material hardship which was so characteristic of families in which the father was absent.

Analysis 2 (including illegitimate, excluding motherless children)

This analysis compared the social adjustment of children living in fatherless families as a result of death, marital breakdown or illegitimacy, with that of their counterparts in two-parent homes. As with the second attainment analysis, each family situation, with the exception of the illegitimate, was then subdivided according to whether the family's social class background was manual or non-manual. Information concerning the mother's education level and current employment situation was also included.

The results of the analysis showed that, as before, when allowance was made for all the other factors which were included, there was little difference in the adjustment of children in the various family situations (Table A13.5). Those living with widowed mothers did not differ significantly from children in two-parent families, while those who were fatherless due to illegitimacy appeared to be as well-adjusted as children living in unbroken families *and* from non-manual backgrounds. Although no comparable social class information was available for the illegitimate children, it is reasonable to suppose that they resembled those from manual rather than non-manual homes in this respect, so that this result might be interpreted as indicating a relatively favourable level of adjustment among this group of children. However, it should be stressed that the number of illegitimate children was small, and although as far as adjustment is concerned they seemed to resemble children from two-parent non-manual homes more than any other group, this estimate must be regarded as somewhat unreliable.

There is abundant research evidence (e.g. Davie, Butler and Goldstein, 1972) to show that, using measures such as the one employed here, children from a non-manual background are on the whole better adjusted than those from manual homes, and as far as those living with both parents were concerned, this was also the case in the present study. It was *not* so, however, among the children living in fatherless families. In fact, although the differences were not statistically significant, there was actually a tendency for those from manual homes to be seen as slightly *better* adjusted, whether the cause of the father's absence was death or marital breakdown.

The only significant difference in social adjustment according to family situation was found between children living in non-manual homes with both parents present and all those who were fatherless as a result of divorce or separation. It is perhaps worth pointing out that the group of children cared for by divorced or separated mothers from a *non-manual* background in fact showed the poorest overall level of adjustment. This finding would seem to link up with others showing the relatively disadvantaged position of these children, not only in relation to material factors in their home background, but also in terms of their parents' interests and aspirations, and their own comparatively poor performance in arithmetic which was described in Chapter Twelve.

Mother working and children's social adjustment

We saw in Chapter Twelve that the relationship between the mother's recent employment experience and her children's attainment varied markedly according to the family situation. Although the pattern was much less pronounced as far as the children's social adjustment was concerned, it was interesting to find that, among the illegitimate children, there was again a tendency for those whose mothers had worked full-time to be seen as better adjusted than the children whose mothers had not been employed, a pattern which was not evident in any of the other groups (Table S13.6).

Behaviour and adjustment at home

While the assessments given by teachers provided an indication of the children's level of adjustment in school, information collected during the health visitors' interview enabled an examination to be made of the children's behaviour as seen by their parents. Parents were asked whether the following descriptions of behaviour could be applied to the study child 'frequently', 'sometimes' or 'never':

a)   has difficulty in settling to anything for more than a few
     moments
b)   prefers to do things on his/her own rather than with others
c)   is bullied by other children
d)   destroys own or others' belongings
e)   is miserable or tearful
f)   is squirmy or fidgety
g)   worries about many things
h)   is irritable, quick to fly off the handle
i)   sucks thumb or finger during the day
j)   is upset by new situations
k)   has twitches or mannerisms of the face, eyes or body
l)   fights with other children
m)   bites nails
n)   is disobedient at home.

In addition, parents were asked to say whether, during the previous
three months, the child concerned had sleep-walked, had bad dreams or
shown reluctance to go to school.

As in all the other areas of our analysis, comparisons were made
between children in different family situations, with those in fatherless
and motherless families subdivided according to the cause of the
situation. The child's sex and social class background were also taken
into account, since both these factors have been shown in earlier studies
to be related to the aspects of behaviour in question (Davie, Butler and
Goldstein, 1972; Pringle, Butler and Davie, 1966). As a result, a very
large number of comparisons were carried out, and it would be
impossible to discuss in detail here the results in each area of behaviour.
What follows, therefore, represents a summary of the main findings to
emerge from the analysis.

The first point to be made is that the great majority of comparisons
did not reveal statistically significant differences between children in
the various family situations (Tables S13.7 (a) (b) and S13.8). In a
number of areas, however, fatherless children as a whole appeared to
exhibit behaviour difficulties rather more frequently than their peers
from two-parent families, although such overall differences often
masked what has become a familiar variation between children whose
fathers had died and those whose parents were divorced or separated.

Boys and girls living with widowed mothers differed very little from
their counterparts in two-parent families as far as their behaviour at
home was concerned. In only one case did a statistically significant
difference emerge: widowed mothers saw their sons as having 'difficulty

in settling to anything' rather more often than mothers in two-parent homes.

In several areas, however, divorced and separated mothers attributed difficulties or disturbed behaviour to their children rather more often than mothers in two-parent families, and this tendency was particularly apparent among girls. Compared with girls in two-parent homes, a greater number of those living with divorced and separated mothers were seen as sometimes or frequently bullied, tearful, fidgety, having difficulty in settling to anything, likely to fight with other children, and having bad dreams.

As far as the illegitimate children were concerned, the behaviour of the girls did not appear to differ much from that of their counterparts in two-parent families, except that they were seen as more often 'fidgety' and prone to fighting and having bad dreams. In several cases, however, illegitimate boys were seen by their mothers as showing *fewer* behaviour difficulties than those in complete families, particularly in the following areas: miserable, tearful; worries about many things; prefers to do things on his/her own. In each case, however, the number of illegitimate children was small, and the differences were not statistically significant.

It is particularly difficult to interpret these findings, for while they may reflect real variations in the behaviour patterns of children in different family situations, it should be remembered that it was the mother's own *perceptions* which were used as an indicator of their children's behaviour. It could well be that there were variations in the attitudes and perceptions of mothers in different family circumstances. Mothers on their own, for example, might be more anxious about their children's behaviour than mothers in unbroken homes, and more on the look-out for any sign of disturbance which might be seen as reflecting the family's anomalous situation. The circumstances surrounding marital breakdown, while increasing the emotional vulnerability of the children, might also make divorced and separated mothers particularly anxious about the effects of the situation and more ready than other mothers to perceive problem behaviour in their children. Evidence from the follow-up study (Ferri and Robinson, 1976) provides some support for this suggestion, as does the Department of Health and Social Security report 'Families Receiving Supplementary Benefit' (1972). Two-fifths of the lone mothers in this sample said that their children's behaviour caused them 'special' worries; some saw their children as too aggressive, others felt they were too withdrawn. Sometimes the anxiety focussed on the relationship between mother and child. In all cases, however, there seemed to be an implicit fear of the adverse effects of the father's absence.

With regard to the illegitimate children, here again the findings may point to real differences in behaviour and/or they may reflect an unwillingness, conscious or unconscious, among mothers in difficult social circumstances to perceive behaviour problems in their children which could be seen as a criticism of their family situation.

The behaviour ratings given to children living in motherless families showed a similar pattern to those of the illegitimate. Motherless girls differed little from those living in two-parent homes, but boys without a mother appeared to show fewer difficulties than their counterparts in unbroken homes. This tendency was apparent in several areas of behaviour and reached statistical significance in the case of 'worries about many things' and 'disobedient'.

It should be remembered that in the case of the motherless group we were looking at the *father's* ratings of their children's behaviour, while in the two-parent sample the assessment was (usually) made by the mother; so that the findings reported above could reflect differences in the perceptions of fathers and mothers. It could perhaps be that, as a result of differences in parent-child relationships and interactions, fathers are, on the whole, rather less sensitive to or critical of children's behaviour than mothers — or simply less likely to mention problems in an interview situation. There is little reason to suppose that motherless children would have experienced fewer behaviour difficulties than those in two-parent homes, and it seems that the lone father might need to cultivate an increased awareness of his children's feelings and problems in his role as the sole source of parental comfort and support. Comments from fathers in the follow-up study (Ferri and Robinson, 1976) indicated that it was the role of comforter and provider of emotional support that many found particularly difficult.

Family situation and enuresis

Persistent bed-wetting among children who would normally be expected to have achieved bladder control is seen by many as symptomatic of emotional disturbance of some kind. Although there is a lack of consensus regarding the underlying cause or causes, the condition is clearly one which is likely to arouse anxiety and distress, both in the children concerned and in their parents.

Using the information from the National Survey of Health and Development, Douglas, (1970), reported that family breakdown was associated with a relatively high level of enuresis at each age studied (up to fifteen years)) except when it was due to the death of the father. He also found that among children living with divorced and separated mothers alone, the level of enuresis fell by the age of eleven to be comparable to that among children in two-parent families.

When the children in our own sample were eleven, parents were asked whether or not the child had been completely dry at night during the preceding month. From the information obtained, comparisons were made between children living in different family situations.

No differences emerged in the prevalence of bedwetting among girls living with widowed or divorced or separated mothers and those in two-parent homes, either overall or when social class and cause of family situation were taken into account. One per cent, two per cent and three per cent respectively, had wet their beds at some time during the preceding month (Table S13.9 (a)). Motherless girls and those who were fatherless due to illegitimacy contained rather higher proportions who had wet their beds (five per cent and seven per cent respectively), but in each case the actual numbers involved (only two in each group) were too small for statistical comparisons to be made.

No differences were found between boys whose mothers were absent (five per cent) and those in two-parent homes (six per cent). Boys in fatherless families, however, showed a rather higher level of bedwetting (ten per cent) and, in contrast to Douglas' findings referred to above, the problem seemed to be most common among those living with widowed mothers (12 per cent).

A similar pattern was found among boys at both social class levels, although the actual number of enuretic boys in the fatherless group was very small, and among those from manual backgrounds, the difference between fatherless and two-parent boys did not reach significance (Tables S13.9 (b) (c)).

During the first National Child Development Study follow-up, when the children were seven, details were obtained about the number who had wet their beds at night after the age of five. This information enabled long-term comparisons to be made between children in different family situations.

No differences were found between girls in fatherless and two-parent families, but the findings showed that bedwetting was more likely to have been a *continuing* problem among boys who had lost their father than among their peers in unbroken homes. Two-thirds (66 per cent) of the boys in two-parent families who had been enuretic after five years of age were dry at night by the time they were eleven. The corresponding figure for fatherless boys, however, was only 38 per cent (Table S13.10).

It also appeared that a relatively high number of fatherless boys (87 per cent) who were enuretic at eleven had already been reported as wetting their beds four years earlier, although the proportion was not significantly greater than that found among boys from two-parent homes (70 per cent) (Table S13.11). There was no evidence, however, that the *onset* of bedwetting between seven and eleven in children who were previously dry was any more frequent among fatherless boys than among those in complete families (Table S13.12). For a large proportion of fatherless boys, therefore, enuresis had preceded rather than followed the actual loss of the father, so that family breakdown would seem to be associated with the *persistence* of the condition rather than giving rise to it.

Although the overall difference in the level of enuresis between fatherless and two-parent boys was statistically significant, it should be stressed that, in numerical terms, it was quite small (i.e. 10 per cent as against six per cent). It is also worth pointing out that such a difference might well be reduced if other relevant factors were taken into account.

Whether or not the problem of bedwetting in boys can be linked to the absence of the father *per se*, it seems probable that in the fatherless family such a condition would be particularly distressing to the mother and children concerned, in view of the wide range of other problems and anxieties which their family circumstances have been shown to generate.

Summary and conclusions

In this chapter we have been looking at the children's social adjustment in school as seen by their teachers, and in the parent's reports of various aspects of their behaviour at home. As far as adjustment in school was concerned, children from one-parent families appeared overall to be less well adjusted than their peers in two-parent homes. However, our analysis showed that this difference was related, not to the absence of a parent *per se* but to factors associated with both a one-parent situation *and* relatively poor adjustment. There was thus little evidence that the loss or absence of a parent *in itself* was adversely related to the social adjustment of the children concerned.

There was however, a tendency for children living with divorced or separated mothers to be seen as rather less well-adjusted in school than children from two-parent homes, and the mothers of these children were slightly more likely than other mothers to perceive problems in their behaviour at home, in particular among their daughters.

Boys who had lost their father, (but *not* those whose mothers were absent) were more likely to be enuretic at the age of eleven than were their counterparts in unbroken families, and this also appeared to be a more *persistent* problem among the fatherless boys than among those who had not experienced any break in their family.

On the whole, however, any differences in behaviour and adjustment between children in one and two-parent families were small in magnitude and our findings have suggested that the absence of a parent had not in itself had the overwhelmingly detrimental effect so often attributed to it.

It would clearly be nonsensical to suggest that the shock and distress of bereavement or of the parents' separation had had no effect upon the children concerned. Our own follow-up study (Ferri and Robinson, 1976) provided some insight into the kinds of problems and difficulties which many children had experienced during and after the break in the family. Inevitably, in a large-scale study such as this, the measures of behaviour and adjustment available were relatively crude, and covered a limited number of areas. Furthermore, a subsequent investigation of the same groups of children would be required in order to assess whether family situation is related to social and emotional problems in later adolescence. With these reservations in mind, however, it can be concluded that the majority of the eleven-year-old children had, on the whole, adjusted to their family circumstances, and that any emotional disturbance associated with the actual loss or absence of a parent had been largely overcome.

Chapter Fourteen

Children's aspirations

In an achievement-orientated, 'mobile' society, an individual's level of
aspirations and motivation will play an important part in determining
his or her 'success'. These attitudes will be shaped to a considerable
extent, and from an early age, by factors in the family and home
background. It was felt important, therefore, to try to find out whether
the family circumstances of the children in our sample appeared to be
related in any way to the aspirations which the children themselves held
for their future.

Just as few studies have looked at the attitudes of lone parents
towards their children's education and training, so only a very small
number have investigated any aspect of the children's own hopes for
their future. There is some evidence from studies in the United States
that a disproportionate number of high school and college drop-outs
come from broken homes, (Gregory, 1965; Lanier, 1949; Miller, Saleem
and Bryce, 1964). Gregory found that the rate of premature leaving was
particularly high among students who had been brought up by one
parent of the opposite sex to themselves. Other studies have suggested
that children from one-parent families tend to be less successful in
terms of their actual occupational achievement than similarly qualified
young people from unbroken homes (Duncan and Duncan, 1969;
Kriesberg, 1970).

The information collected during the second National Child Development Study follow-up provided a number of measures of the
eleven-year-old children's feelings about their future which enabled
comparisons to be made between those in different family situations.
From a questionnaire completed by the children themselves in school,
details were available about their hopes for their subsequent education
and training and about the actual jobs which they wanted to obtain.
The children were also asked to write an essay describing their lives as
adults, and this material provided, among other things, some indication
of their attitudes towards marriage and having children of their own.

Further training and employment

One of the questions put to the children concerned their plans after leaving school. Clearly, it would be unreasonable to expect eleven-year-old children to be well-informed about the range of possibilities open to them, and so they were simply asked to choose between the two broad categories of further full-time study or immediate employment. Even so, almost half of the children concerned said that they did not yet know what they wanted to do.

Although in some groups the numbers giving a positive response were rather small, it was decided to look at the answers given by children in different family situations to see whether the absence of a parent was related to the aspirations expressed. Boys and girls were studied separately, partly in order to see whether parental situation affected the two sexes in different ways, and partly because the responses of boys and girls tended, in any case, to be very different. Boys were less likely than girls to choose further full-time study, and were more likely to opt for immediate employment, probably because the actual occupations chosen by many boys would involve an apprenticeship of some kind. As in other areas of the inquiry, children from manual and non-manual home backgrounds were also looked at separately.

i) Fatherless boys

The most marked difference in the aspirations of the various groups of boys in the sample lay in the relatively high proportion of those in fatherless homes who intended to go straight into a job after leaving school (35 per cent compared with 24 per cent of the boys in two-parent families) (Table S14.1 (a)). Boys who had lost their father as a result of marital breakdown contained the highest number choosing immediate employment (40 per cent), followed by those whose father had died (34 per cent). The proportion among the fatherless illegitimate boys (23 per cent) was similar to that found in the two-parent group, but the number involved here was very small.

The tendency for fatherless boys to opt for a job straight away was especially marked among those from non-manual backgrounds (48 per cent as against only 17 per cent among boys from unbroken non-manual homes) (Table S14.1 (b)). In fact, among the boys from fatherless homes, the number choosing to go out to work immediately after leaving school was actually higher at the non-manual than at the manual level (32 per cent), whereas among boys from two-parent homes the reverse was, predictably, the case. As far as boys from manual homes were concerned, there was little difference between widows' sons (22 per cent) and those living with both parents (27 per cent) but boys from families broken by divorce or separation were again more likely to intend to get a job straight away (39 per cent) (Table S14.1 (c)).

Boys in two parent families were rather more likely than those from fatherless homes to hope to carry on with full-time study after leaving school, (27 per cent and 22 per cent respectively), and among those from non-manual homes the difference was statistically significant (36 per cent as against 23 per cent).

ii) Fatherless girls

As far as the girls were concerned the picture was rather different, for there was an overall similarity in the aspirations expressed by those in fatherless and two-parent families. Nineteen per cent of the former and 17 per cent of the latter indicated that they proposed to take a job immediately after leaving school (Table S14.2 (a)). Within the fatherless group, however, daughters of divorced or separated mothers and girls who were illegitimate were rather more likely than widows' daughters to choose to go out to work straightaway (22 per cent, 21 per cent and 11 per cent respectively), although the difference was not statistically significant.

The number of girls proposing to carry on with full-time study did not differ significantly according to their family situation; altogether 32 per cent of those living with both parents and 34 per cent of the fatherless girls chose this alternative.

It would seem from the above findings that, as far as the aspirations measured here are concerned, boys were more affected than girls by the absence of their father. Without further information it is impossible to trace the actual ways in which the attitudes of these boys had been influenced by their home circumstances. One likely explanation, however, lies in the financial position of families without a father, and the need for children in such families to begin as soon as possible to contribute to the household income. This would no doubt weigh particularly heavily upon the sons concerned, who may feel themselves under some pressure to take on the role of male breadwinner. The fact that girls in families which were fatherless due to marital breakdown or illegitimacy were also rather more likely than widows' daughters to choose early employment offers some support for this explanation, for it was among the former two groups that the pressures of economic hardship were shown in Chapter Seven to be particularly severe.

iii) Motherless children

Next, an examination was made of the aspirations expressed by the motherless children in the sample. Unfortunately, in view of the small number of motherless children and the large proportion of those who did not yet know what they wanted to do after leaving school, it was not possible to take into account both the sex of the child and social class background.

It was interesting to discover, however, that while there appeared to be little overall difference between motherless children and those living with both parents, this was due to a marked variation within the motherless group according to the reason for the mother's absence. Children whose fathers were divorced or separated were much more likely than those whose mothers had died to hope to continue their full-time education after leaving school and this was particularly marked amongst the boys (46 per cent and 13 per cent respectively (Table S14.1 (a)). It might be the case that this difference was linked to the relatively higher level of interest and involvement with their children which was found among divorced and separated fathers when their own attitudes and aspirations were examined (Chapter Eleven).

The children's future occupations

As already mentioned above, a projective essay was one of the items contained in the test booklet administered to the children in school. The children were asked to 'imagine that you are now 25 years old. Write about the life you are leading, your interests, your home life and your work at the age of 25'. Over 80 per cent of the children who wrote a description of their life as an adult gave sufficient information about the work they expected to be doing for the occupations mentioned to be classified. It was decided to look at the actual jobs described by children in various family groups to see whether there were any differences in the status level of the occupations to which they aspired. As the numbers mentioning each individual occupation were very small, the analysis was simplified by comparing the total number in each group who referred to 'high' status jobs. These included professional/managerial and intermediate,[1] as well as all other non-manual occupations.

As before, separate analyses were carried out for boys and girls. In each case, the findings showed no differences between children from fatherless, motherless or two-parent families, either overall, or when social class background or cause of family breakdown was taken into account.

i) Boys

Among the boys, 36 per cent of those living with both parents mentioned a non-manual occupation, compared with 33 per cent in

---

1 According to the Registrar General's 1966 classification of occupations.

fatherless and 35 per cent in motherless homes (Table S14.3 (a)). By far the most popular single occupation among boys was skilled manual work of some kind, with more than one boy in every four opting for this (Table S14.5). The next most frequently mentioned occupations were professional/managerial work or sportsman (13 per cent in each case) reflecting perhaps the rather unrealistic aspirations of boys at this age which have also been reported in other studies (e.g. Barker Lunn, 1970).

ii) Girls

Sixty-eight per cent of the girls from two-parent homes mentioned a non-manual job, as against 66 per cent in fatherless and 59 per cent in motherless families (Table S14.4 (a)). The most frequently mentioned job among the girls was that of teacher (17 per cent) followed by typing or other clerical work (15 per cent). Nursing (13 per cent) and personal service jobs (13 per cent) were also highly chosen, and these four occupational categories together accounted for well over half of the girls in the sample (Table S14.5).

Thus, although it had been found that fatherless children, especially fatherless boys, were more likely than those with both parents to expect to start work immediately after leaving school, the present findings show no evidence of lower aspirations among these children in terms of the actual jobs which they hoped to attain. Whether or not they do subsequently achieve the same occupational status as their counterparts from unbroken families is, of course, a question which only a future investigation of the same group of children could attempt to answer.

The children's views of their future

It was decided to carry out a simple content analysis of the projective essays written by a sample of the children in the present study, to see whether their family circumstances were associated in any way with the ideas expressed about other aspects of their future adult lives.

All the motherless children for whom essay material was available were included, as were all illegitimate children living in fatherless families. Because of limitations in time and resources, the investigation of the remaining fatherless children was confined to those who had lost their father since the age of seven. For the purpose of comparison, a further sample of 300 children from two-parent families was drawn at random, after matching as far as possible for family size.

A rough check was carried out on the ability level of the children in the one and two-parent groups. Any wide differences in ability might make comparisons of doubtful validity, since less able children would tend to write less, thus reducing the likelihood of any particular factor being mentioned. However, an examination of the proportion in each group falling in the bottom 30 per cent of the total ability distribution revealed no significant differences.

A number of areas were covered in the content analysis, including any mention of the children's own parents and siblings, reference to where and with whom they expected to be living, and rather more subjective assessments of 'achievement motivation' and the overall impression of satisfaction (or otherwise) with the lives envisaged. Our chief interest, however, lay in the children's references to marriage and having a family of their own. It was felt important to try to discover whether family background at eleven was related in any way to the children's views concerning their own future as wives, husbands and parents. For, example, would children who had experienced the distress of a family broken by marital disharmony be less attracted by the prospect of marriage and family life themselves? And what would be the feelings of illegitimate children who had never known a home life based on marriage and two parents?

a) Marriage

A comparison was made of the number of children in each family situation who indicated in their essays that they would be married or intending to get married by the age of 25. The figures showed that this topic was more likely to feature in the girls' essays (57 per cent altogether) than in those of the boys (46 per cent). Among both boys and girls, however, fatherless children were rather less likely than those in two-parent families to make a positive reference to marriage, although only when the two sexes were combined did the difference reach statistical significance. Altogether 56 per cent of children in two-parent families saw themselves as married or intending to marry compared with 47 per cent of fatherless children (Table S14.6). The lowest proportion of all (only 37 per cent) was found among children who were fatherless as a result of illegitimacy.

No differences were found between motherless boys and those in two-parent homes — 50 per cent in each case expected or intended to be married. Although there was a slight difference between motherless girls (49 per cent) and their counterparts in unbroken families (62 per cent), the number in the former group was small and the difference was not statistically significant.

Among the children who did *not* make a positive reference to marriage the great majority made no mention of the subject at all. That is to say, relatively few children stated categorically that they did not intend to get married, and the proportions among those in fatherless, motherless and two-parent families were very similar (11 per cent, 11 per cent and 8 per cent respectively). It was interesting to find, however, that the highest proportion of children who said that they would not get married were found in families broken by divorce and separation (12 per cent among those living with their mothers and 16 per cent of those cared for by their fathers), although in neither case was the number significantly greater than that in other groups.

b) Children

A study was also made of the number of children who referred in their essays to having a family of their own when they grew up. Not surprisingly, this too was a topic more frequently mentioned by girls — 49 per cent altogether referred to having children compared with 38 per cent of the boys. In this area, however, rather more marked differences emerged between children in the various family situations. Only 37 per cent of fatherless children indicated they they expected to be parents themselves compared with 50 per cent of those in two-parent families, and this difference was especially marked among the girls (41 per cent and 57 per cent respectively) (Table S14.7). Although all three fatherless groups were rather less likely than children in two-parent homes to refer to having children of their own, the lowest proportion (29 per cent) was again found among children who were illegitimate.

Neither boys nor girls in motherless families differed significantly in this respect from their counterparts in two-parent homes, although a rather lower proportion (41 per cent) of the motherless children indicated that they would be parents by the age of 25.

It is perhaps prudent to point out that the indirect measures of attitudes and expectations which have been employed here are of questionable validity and reliability, and that any interpretation of the above findings must be cautious and tentative. However, the differences which have emerged do suggest a possible relationship between children's family experiences and their views of their own future as members of a family. This seems particularly likely in the case of fatherless illegitimate children who, never having experienced a 'normal' two-parent family situation themselves, appeared least likely to see marriage and children of their own as a salient feature of their adult lives. However inconclusive the findings reported here may be, they would seem to point to a need for further research into this largely unexplored, but obviously crucial, area of children's development.

Summary and conclusions

This chapter has looked at the relationship between family situation and three aspects of children's aspirations and expectations: 1) length of education and training, 2) type of occupation chosen, and 3) their views of their own future as members of a family.

The findings have indicated that, in families where the father was absent, a relatively high proportion of boys expected to go out to work immediately after leaving school, and that this tendency was particularly marked among those from non-manual backgrounds and homes broken by divorce and separation. It was not possible from the available data to assess how far such expectations reflected the absence of paternal influence in terms of the fathers' own attitudes and aspirations, and/or possible differences in the attitudes of mothers on their own and those in complete families. It does seem likely, however, that at least a contributory factor was the material disadvantage suffered by fatherless families, which would no doubt engender direct and indirect pressure on the children concerned to contribute as soon as possible to the family income.

The most striking finding to emerge with regard to the aspirations of motherless children in this area was the difference *within* this group. Children in families broken by divorce or separation were much more likely to want to prolong their full-time education than those whose mother had died. It was suggested that these findings might link up with the differences reported earlier in the attitudes of widowers and divorced or separated fathers.

In spite of the association between family situation and expected length of education and training, no differences appeared between children in one and two-parent families when a study was made of the actual occupations which they expected to obtain.

Fatherless (particularly illegitimate) children were found to be rather less likely than those in two-parent families to mention marriage and having children of their own in their description of the lives they would be leading at the age of 25. These results, based on indirect measures, must be treated with caution, and we must await future research for insight into the children's actual experiences with regard to marriage and parenthood. However, the present findings would seem to suggest a possible relationship between family situation and the development of attitudes which would clearly be of importance in the later lives and happiness of the children concerned.

The present study has been able to look only at one or two broad and very different aspects of the aspirations and expectations of the children in our sample. In view of the established importance of such attitudes for subsequent development, however, the albeit tentative findings of this investigation might serve to draw attention to this as a fruitful area for further study, not only of the effects of family breakdown on the development of children, but of the part played by all kinds of factors in the family situation in the formation and modification of such attitudes and expectations.

Chapter Fifteen

Family situation and
aspects of health

We have now seen how the school attainment, social adjustment and aspirations of children in one-parent families compared with that of their peers in unbroken homes. One final aspect of the children's development remains to be investigated, namely, their physical health and welfare.

Few studies to date have looked at the relationship between family situation and health, and little is known about the physical development of children in one-parent families. Rowntree (1955) using data collected for the National Survey of Health and Development, found somewhat poorer standards of child care among broken than among complete families in terms of clothing and cleanliness, although there was little difference between children from the two groups as far as average height and weight were concerned. Hunt *et al.* (1973) studying assessments made by parents, found little evidence that the absence of a father or mother had adversely affected the health of the children concerned. The study by the Department of Health and Social Security (1972) of families receiving Supplementary Benefit found that 20 per cent of fatherless children had been admitted to hospital because of illness compared with only 12 per cent of those in two-parent families, although the figures could well reflect differences in family circumstances rather than in the actual prevalence of serious illness. In the United States, Burchinal (1964) compared the school attendance rates of adolescents in different family situations, and found the highest level of absence among boys who were being cared for by an unsupported mother.

At each National Child Development study follow-up, a great deal of information was collected concerning the medical history and physical development of the children in the sample. However, limitations of time and resources made it necessary to confine the present analysis to an examination of the rates of school absence among children in different family situations. Douglas and Ross (1968) and Fogelman and Richardson (1974) have drawn attention to the importance of regular school attendance for educational achievement and progress, and any tendency for children from one-parent families to show a disproportionately high level of absence would seem likely to add to the disadvantages from which they have already been shown to suffer.

Family situation and absence from school

During their interview with the health visitor, parents were asked whether the child in the study had been absent from school due to illness for one week or more during the previous year. Using the information obtained, comparisons were made between children in different family situations, with separate analyses carried out for boys and girls.

i) Boys

As far as the boys were concerned, there were no differences in the amount of school absence between those in fatherless and two-parent families, either overall or when allowance was made for social class background. Sixty-two per cent of the fatherless and 64 per cent of the two-parent boys had been away from school for less than one week during the year in question (table S15.1(a)). There was a slight tendency for illegitimate boys to have been away more often (only 52 per cent had less than one week's absence) but they were few in number and did not differ significantly from boys in two-parent homes.

Motherless boys, on the other hand, were found to have a significantly *better* record of attendance than their counterparts from unbroken homes. Altogether 82 per cent had had less than one week off school, and, although the numbers were small here also, the same pattern was found when the cause of the mother's absence was taken into account.

ii) Girls

With regard to the fatherless girls the picture was rather different. Only 54 per cent had been absent from school for less than one week compared with 60 per cent of girls from two-parent families (table S15.2 (a)). There was no difference among the fatherless group according to the reason for the father's absence, and the same trend was apparent at both social class levels (table S15.2 (b) and (c)).

In contrast to the fatherless girls, there was a tendency for those in motherless homes, like their male counterparts, to have a rather *better* attendance record than girls in unbroken families (66 per cent and 60 per cent respectively had had less than one week off school), and among those from manual backgrounds the difference approached statistical significance (75 per cent and 58 per cent respectively.)

Although none of the differences mentioned above was very large, the results of this analysis suggest that family situation *is* related to school absence, but that the nature of the relationship depends upon the sex of the children concerned and upon which parent is absent.

What factors could account for the differences reported above? Did fatherless girls suffer from poorer health than girls in two-parent homes? It should perhaps be pointed out that the relationship between illness and absence from school is not necessarily a straightforward one, and that, although the question put to parents specifically concerned absence for health reasons, it is possible that other factors played a part in the decision to keep a child away from school. Douglas and Ross (1968) for example, found that the illness of either parent was related to girls, rather than boys, being kept at home to help cope with the situation. Marsden (1969) also reported instances among his sample of fatherless families of children staying away from school to look after a sick mother. School children were kept at home in preference to older, working siblings in order to avoid the additional financial hardship of lost wages. It seems possible that factors such as these could at least partly account for the relatively high absence rate among the fatherless girls in the present study.

But what about the motherless children? Was their health in fact *better* than that of their peers in two-parent families? Here again, it may be that school attendance in itself presents an inaccurate picture of the children's general level of health. Just as some children may stay away from school for reasons other than illness, so it may be that others go to school when they are in fact unwell and would be better off at home. In view of the particular problems facing the motherless family, this might well account, at least to some extent, for the comparatively low level of absence found among these children. The great majority of the lone fathers in the sample were working full-time and it would clearly be difficult in most cases to arrange for the day care of a sick child. Our follow up study (Ferri and Robinson, 1976) provided vivid illustrations of the problems and anxieties which such a situation presented to lone parents of either sex who went out to work. George and Wilding (1972) found that one in five of the lone fathers in their study had taken time off work at some time to look after children who were ill, but this had clearly presented problems such as loss of earnings and, more seriously, placing their employment situation at risk. Under such circumstances it would not be surprising if fathers on their own allowed children to go to school when suffering from symptoms or ailments which in a 'normal' family situation might have kept them at home.

Our findings concerning the school attendance of motherless children show a similar trend to those quoted by Hunt *et al.* (1973). In their study, lone fathers were less likely to report poor health among their children than were mothers on their own or in unbroken families, although, as the authors pointed out: 'it is possible that fathers are less knowledgeable about children's health than mothers or less inclined to become alarmed over comparatively minor ailments.'

Ill health in any member of a one-parent family can clearly provoke a major crisis in a situation where time, energy and resources are already stretched to the limit. As our follow-up study (Ferri and Robinson, 1976) showed, even in families which had largely avoided illness, the very thought of falling sick and the problems which this would entail, was a perennial nightmare to many unsupported parents. Illness in the parent themselves could mean not only that crucial earnings might be forfeited, but also that the children would be deprived of their sole provider of care and support.

Family situation and the parents' health

The parent's health would seem to be of major importance for the day-to-day functioning of the one-parent family. In view of this, it was decided to turn our attention from the children for a moment, and look at the recent health record of the parents in different family situations. During the interview parents had been asked whether they had suffered from any chronic or serious disability or ill health since the study child's seventh birthday (i.e. a period of about four years). From the information obtained, diagnoses and classifications were carried out by medical members of the research team.

The findings showed that mothers on their own were more than twice as likely as those in unbroken families to have been chronically or seriously ill or disabled (13 per cent as against six per cent), with the highest rates found among mothers who had been divorced or separated (15 per cent) (Table S15.3). Information was also available about the nature of the illness or disability suffered. In general the numbers involved were too small for detailed comparisons to be made, but it was striking to note the relatively high prevalence of psychiatric illness among mothers whose marriage had broken down. Among this group, 42 per cent of those who had suffered from a chronic or serious illness or disability had experienced some kind of psychiatric disturbance, compared with 27 per cent of mothers in two-parent families, and only 22 per cent of widows (Table S15.4). Although no further details were available, it seems likely that in many cases, the disturbance was related to the nature of the family breakdown itself, either as a contributory factor or in response to the situation. It is also reasonable to assume that such illness would be of a relatively long-term nature and likely to be both indicative and productive of strains and tension among the remaining members of the family.

Altogether 11 per cent of the fathers on their own reported conditions which were classified as serious or chronic illness or disability. This compared with seven per cent among fathers in unbroken families, a difference which was not statistically significant (Table S15.5). There was no evidence that the cause of the family breakdown was related in any way to the prevalence of illness or disability among lone fathers, although the numbers in each group were very small. As a result of the limited numbers, it was not possible to carry out any analysis of the conditions involved.

Summary and conclusions

This brief investigation has shown that family situation appeared to be related to the pattern of school absence shown by the children in the present study. Motherless children had a rather better record of attendance than those in two-parent families, while boys from fatherless homes did not differ from their counterparts living with both parents. Fatherless girls, however, were more likely to have been absent from school for a week or more than girls in two-parent families.

Further investigation would be required to confirm and explain these differences, but it might tentatively be suggested that the circumstances of the motherless family made it less practicable for such children to stay at home when there was no adult to care for them, and that some may have gone to school when they were less than one hundred per cent fit. Whether, if substantiated, such a tendency would be found to be detrimental in its effects, is a further question beyond the scope of this study.

It would seem from our findings that fatherless girls either suffered from somewhat poorer health than girls in two-parent families, or that they sometimes stayed away from school for reasons other than sickness. Previous research has suggested that girls may be kept off school to care for sick parents or siblings, a situation which seems particularly likely to occur in the fatherless family, where such illness could present a serious emergency. The peculiar circumstances of the fatherless family suggest other possible reasons for a higher absence rate among its daughters. The isolated position of the lone mother, for example, might make her more ready to keep a daughter at home for assistance or company on a relatively slight pretext. Perhaps too, lone mothers are more anxious about their children's health and may thus be more likely to keep them away from school for minor complaints, although why such anxiety should be confined to girls is not clear.

On the whole, there is little evidence to suggest that children in one-parent families suffered from poorer health than those in two-parent homes, at least as far as absence from school was concerned. Unsupported parents, however, did appear to be more prone to chronic or serious illness or disability than their counterparts in unbroken families, with as many as one in seven of the divorced and separated mothers having suffered in some way in the previous four years. When one considers the burdensome responsibilities facing lone parents, and the increased anxiety and problems which such illness is bound to produce, it seems likely that the effects may well be far-reaching and severe, threatening the material, physical and emotional welfare of both parents and children.

Chapter Sixteen

Summary and conclusions

The aim of this study has been to compare the environment and development of a nationally representative sample of children from one and two-parent families.

Over the past few years a number of reports and mounting publicity have drawn attention to the problems and handicaps facing families which lose a parent, culminating in the publication of the report of the Finer Committee (1974), which has recommended measures designed to alleviate their difficulties. The information available from the National Child Development Study however, has made it possible for the first time to assess the extent of material and environmental disadvantage among a representative sample of *children* who lack one parent and, by making due allowance for such disadvantage, to measure the 'effect' of the family situation upon their educational, social and psychological development.

The main findings in each of the areas of inquiry included in the investigation have been summarized at the end of the relevant chapter, and to avoid repetition, they have not been included again here. However, there are one or two more general points arising from the research which should perhaps be re-stated in drawing this report to a conclusion.

Firstly, in assessing the extent of material disadvantage suffered by children in one-parent families, the sex of the absent parent and the cause of the situation were found to be of crucial importance. Problems of financial hardship and poor accommodation were less frequently found among motherless families than among those in which the father was absent. Within the fatherless group, the death of the father was less likely to have brought such difficulties than the breakdown of marriage or being the mother of an illegitimate child. What is even more important, however, especially for those concerned with the alleviation of the problems facing one-parent families, is that the position of motherless families and those headed by widowed mothers was only *relatively* more favourable. Compared with children living in unbroken families, *all* groups which lacked a parent tended to suffer from a disadvantage in terms of their material environment and standard of living.

A major aim of our study was to investigate the effects of their family experience upon children's development, particularly in terms of their educational attainment, behaviour and adjustment. The results of the analyses carried out showed that, overall, children in one-parent families had a lower level of attainment in school and were less well adjusted than their peers from unbroken homes. However, the findings also indicated the extent to which such differences were related to the family situation *per se* or to disadvantaging factors which were found to be *associated* with the absence of a parent.

For example, after allowance had been made for handicapping factors in their background, children cared for by widowed mothers showed on the whole little sign of having been adversely affected by their bereavement. This seems to suggest that where breaks occur in an otherwise stable and united family, the children gradually overcome any initial disturbance and adapt to their changed family circumstances.

Losing a father through divorce or separation however, appeared to have produced more lasting effects, and our findings offered some support for Rutter's (1972), suggestion that it may be 'distortion' rather than 'disruption' of family relationships which is detrimental to children's development. The period of stress and conflict which was likely to have preceded the final breakdown in the family may well have been the key factor in the rather poorer development shown among these fatherless children even after other disadvantaging factors had been taken into account.

The small group of fatherless illegitimate children, like those of widows, showed few adverse effects due to their family situation as such, *after* allowance had been made for the handicaps associated with it. It is perhaps worth pointing out that these children had not 'lost' a father in the same sense as the others in the sample, and, from the information available to the study, appeared to have experienced a fairly stable, although materially disadvantaged, home environment.

Although our sample of motherless children was also small, the findings showed that the absence of the mother had, in itself, had an adverse effect on the children's development, and that this was the case regardless of the reason for her absence. It would be rash perhaps, to interpret this as conclusive evidence of the relative importance of the mother-child relationship, particularly in a social context in which fathers, whether lone parents or not, are increasingly taking on aspects of a role which was formerly confined to the mother. While the role itself may well be crucial to the child's welfare and development, it is perhaps also true that the mother is not necessarily the only person who can adequately fulfil it.

Two further points should perhaps be stressed in relation to the effects of family situation on children's development. Firstly, wherever adverse 'effects' were found to be associated with the absence of a parent, the actual differences between the children concerned and those in two-parent families were quite small. In fact the influence of the family situation itself was much weaker than that of other factors such as low social class, large family size, and limited parental aspirations. One particularly striking finding to emerge from the analysis was the importance of the factor relating to economic hardship (defined in terms of receipt of free school meals) in 'accounting for' the relatively poor performance of children from fatherless families.

It should also be emphasized that we have been concerned with *average* differences between the groups of children in the sample. Not *all* children living with lone fathers or divorced and separated mothers will have done less well in school than their peers in 'normal' family circumstances. In fact the relatively small magnitude of the *average* difference between the various groups suggests that a great many lone parents had been highly 'successful' in bringing up their children singlehanded.

The second point to be made however, gives rather less cause for optimism. Our assessment of the children's progress and development involved the use of statistical techniques to isolate the 'effects' of family situation from those of other relevant factors. If this had not been done, children from one-parent families would have appeared to do relatively less well, since they tended to suffer more than two-parent children from other disadvantaging factors. Teachers, however, and others involved with children in a practical setting, are not in a position to 'weigh up' all the variables which might be influencing a child's performance. There is thus a risk that, where teachers are aware of children's home circumstances, the apparently poor showing of many from one-parent homes could be attributed to their family situation as such, thus giving rise to a self-fulfilling prophecy based on low expectations of children known to come from one-parent families.

The question of more general social attitudes towards the one-parent family has not been discussed in any great detail in this report, since the information available concerned only the parents and children themselves. This is a particularly important area however, for the attitudes which the family meets, and the treatment it receives in the wider social context will play a crucial role in its ability to recover from the unhappy experience of losing a parent, and to come to terms with its changed circumstances.

Evidence from our own follow-up study however, (Ferri and Robinson, 1976) has shown that, far from being conducive to the re-integration of one-parent families into the social fabric, the ambivalent and often negative attitudes which society adopts toward such families serves only to isolate them and add to the multiple difficulties which they already face.

Could it be that such attitudes are reflected in the apparent total inadequacy of the supportive services offered to one-parent families by official agencies? In spite of the myriad problems facing the families in the present sample, only a minority appeared to have had any contact at all with the personal social services. All too frequently it appears that assistance from official sources is not forthcoming until the problems of such families reach crisis proportions. The needs of one-parent families, however, are of a day-to-day, continuing and long-term nature.

Bringing up children singlehanded is an arduous task, both physically and mentally. Help is needed, not only in providing for the family's material welfare which is so gravely threatened by the loss of a parent, but also in offering guidance, reassurance and moral support to unsupported parents in their lonely role of bringing up children without another adult to share the responsibility. If such help is not forthcoming, the strains and pressures on some lone parents may become so intolerable that they are finally forced to relinquish their burden, resulting in perhaps the worst of all possible outcomes — a no-parent family.

Statistical appendix

Rachel Peto

Analysis of contingency tables

The tables in the appendix give the numbers of children falling into various parental situations, cross-classified by some other characteristic. In every case, we wished to determine whether the distribution over the categories of the characteristic was the same for each parental situation. Comparisons between parental situations have been made pairwise. If the characteristic was dichotomized, we then had a 2 X 2 table and performed the usual X^2 test under the null hypothesis that the two parental situations came from the same population. Where numbers were small, the 'exact' test has been used and a 'P' value quoted. In cases where the characteristic had K categories which were ordered (where $K \geqslant 3$), we wanted to test whether the proportion,

$$\rho_i = \frac{\text{no. children falling into } i\text{th category from parental situation A}}{,, \quad ,, \quad ,, \quad ,, \quad ,, \quad ,, \quad ,, \quad ,, \quad ,, \quad \text{A and B}}$$

$$(i=1, \ldots ., K)$$

had a linear trend over the K levels. (i.e. ρ_is increased or decreased steadily across the ordered K categories). This model may be written as:

$$\rho_i = a + \beta_i$$

The method of analysis appropriate to this model is given by Bhapkar (*Biometrics* 1968, **24**, 329–38)

Adjustment of degrees of freedom for multiple comparisons

The two-way tables give the distributions of each parental situation over the categories of some attribute (suppose there are r categories, with $r \geqslant 2$).

There were four different groups of comparisons between parental situations that we determined might be made before looking at any individual table. The data are always presented in one large table for convenience, but for statistical purposes a particular comparison is regarded as coming from one of four separate tables.

1. Between motherless groups i.e. Death of mother/marital breakdown — r X 2 table with r-1 degrees of freedom.
2. Between two-parent and individual motherless groups — rX3 table with 2(r-1) degrees of freedom.
3. Between fatherless groups i.e. Death of father/marital break-down/illegitimate — rX3 table with 2(r-1) degrees of freedom
4. Between two-parent and individual fatherless groups — rX4 table with 3(r-1) degrees of freedom.
N.B. Sometimes motherless and/or illegitimate groups were omitted from comparisons if their numbers were too small or the attribute was inapplicable to them. In this case the size of the tables and degrees of freedom were adjusted accordingly.

The comparisons have been made pairwise, so each correspond to an rX2 subtable. However since the comparisons made within any of the above four groups were determined to some extent by the data, the degrees of freedom appropriate to the full table from which the sub-table is drawn have been used (given above in each case), not the r-1 D.F. appropriate to the sub-table.

Strictly speaking, an adjustment should also be made for multiple comparisons of two-parent with individual motherless or fatherless groups, but it is small and may be largely ignored. We do, however, express more caution about the nominal significance levels for such comparisons.

This adjustment for multiple comparisons ensured that differences were not claimed as significant when they in fact may have arisen by chance, with no real differences but, say, as the most extreme differences in larger tables having been selected (Gabriel, 1966).

In cases where categories have been combined when found not to differ significantly and then compared with another category, the degrees of freedom used are those appropriate to the uncombined table. However, the total motherless and fatherless groups are combinations of categories but these pre-determined groupings are of intrinsic interest, not suggested by the data. It was therefore appropriate to associate r-1 D.F. with any comparison involving the motherless or fatherless groups. (i.e. when comparing them with each other or either one of them with the two-parent group).

Analyses of association between average test scores and other variables.
In this type of analysis we were interested in the average values of

the test score (reading, maths or social adjustment) cross-classified by other variables. In particular, we wanted to examine the association between the score and parental situation, after making allowance for other 'nuisance' variables (such as social class) and to compare the magnitudes of the 'effects' of parental situation and other variables. We therefore set up a linear model with the test score as dependent variable and parental situation, social class, etc., as independent variables. The analysis of variance technique was used to estimate constants and test various hypotheses about the variables. We were also interested in the possible existence of interactions between parental situation and any other of the independent variables. Accordingly, when suspected interaction terms were tested.

The fitted constants for the levels of each factor sum exactly to zero. In the case of parental situation, various contrasts between particular situations were tested for significance and these results are referred to in the text but not quoted in the appendix.

Tables

In all tables, where tests of significance have been carried out the level of significance is indicated by the following convention:

*	=	significant at the 5% level
* *	=	significant at the 1% level
* * *	=	significant at the 0.1% level

Table A5.3: Parental care situation at seven of children who had i) lost their natural father; ii) lost their natural mother

i) lost natural father

care situation at 7	N	%
mother alone	418	56.9
mother & adoptive or stepfather	229	31.2
mother & other father substitute	87	11.9
total	734	100.0
care situation not known	3	

ii) lost natural mother

care situation at 7	N	%
father alone	33	30.6
father & stepmother	31	28.7
father & other mother substitute	44	40.7
total	108	100.0
care situation not known	3	

lost father/mother by parent alone/not alone at 7: $X^2 = 23.32$ (1df) ***

Table A5.4: Parental care situation at eleven of children who had i) lost their natural father; ii) lost their natural mother

i) lost natural father			*ii) lost natural mother*		
care situation at 11	*N*	*%*	*care situation at 11*	*N*	*%*
mother alone	652	61.1	father alone	98	41.4
mother & adoptive or stepfather	366	34.3	father & stepmother	83	35.0
mother & other father substitute	49	4.6	father & other mother substitute	56	23.6
total	1,067	100.0	*total*	237	100.0

lost father/mother by parent alone/not alone at 11: X^2 = 30.17 (1.d.f.) ***

Table A5.5: Cause of family breakdown among children in one-parent families at eleven

i) lost natural father			*ii) lost natural mother*		
reason for loss of father	*N*	*%*	*reason for loss of mother*	*N*	*%*
death of father	227	34.8	death of mother	48	49.0
marital breakdown	353	54.1	marital breakdown	49	50.0
illegitimacy	58	8.9	other[1]	1	1.0
other[1]	14	2.2			
total:	652	100.0	*total:*	98	100.0

1   Among the fatherless children, two fathers were in prison, two in mental hospitals, two were in the armed forces, and the remainder working away from home, either in Britain or abroad.

The one mother involved was in a mental hospital.

Table A6.2: Social class background of children in different family situations at 11.

Social class:	two parents		fatherless								motherless					
			death of father		marital breakdown		illegitimate		All fatherless		death of mother		marital breakdown		all motherless	
	N	%	N	%	N	%	N	%	N	%	N	%	N	%	N	%
1	503	4.4	9	4.5	6	2.0	0	0.0	15	2.8	2	4.5	1	2.3	3	3.4
2	1575	13.8	26	12.9	26	8.6	1	2.5	53	9.8	2	4.5	3	6.8	5	5.7
3 non-manual	1151	10.1	23	11.4	36	12.0	5	12.5	64	11.8	3	6.8	6	13.6	9	10.2
3 manual	5726	50.3	93	46.3	138	45.8	17	42.5	248	45.8	27	61.4	20	45.5	47	53.4
4	1397	12.3	20	10.0	50	16.6	9	22.5	79	14.6	4	9.1	7	15.9	11	12.5
5	1033	9.1	30	14.9	45	15.0	8	20.0	83	15.3	6	13.6	7	15.9	13	14.8
total	11385	100.0	201	100.0	301	100.0	40	100.0	542	100.0	44	100.0	44	100.0	88	100.0
no information	900		26		52		18		96		4		5		9	

two-parent/fatherless by social class (1,2,3n-m,3m,4,5) χ^2 (linear trend) = 19.86 (1df)***
χ^2 (departure from trend) = 11.20 (4df)*

two-parent/death of father by social class (1,2,3n-m,3m,4,5) χ^2 (linear trend) = 0.25 (3df)
χ^2 (departure from trend) = 6.32 (4df)

two-parent/marital breakdown by social class (1,2,3n-m,3m,4,5) χ^2 (linear trend) = 20.92 (3df)***
χ^2 (departure from trend) = 6.51 (4df)

death of father/marital breakdown by social class (1,2,3n-m,3m,4m5) χ^2 (linear trend) = 4.13 (2df)
χ^2 (departure from trend) = 4.95 (4df)

two-parent/motherless by social class (1,2,3n-m,4,5) χ^2 (linear trend) = 7.81 (1df)**
χ^2 (departure from trend) = 1.29 (3df)

death of mother/marital breakdown by non-manual/manual χ^2 = 0.29 (1df)

Table A6.3: Size of family among children in different family situations at 11

(a) all social classes

no. of children under 21	two parents		fatherless								all fatherless		motherless				all motherless	
			death of father		marital breakdown		illegitimate						death of mother		marital breakdown			
	N	%	N	%	N	%	N	%			N	%	N	%	N	%	N	%
1	1245	10.2	41	18.4	42	12.1	21	41.2			104	16.7	13	27.7	10	20.4	23	24.0
2	4061	33.1	72	32.3	105	30.3	12	23.5			189	30.4	18	38.3	20	40.8	38	39.6
3	3142	25.6	52	23.3	90	25.9	7	13.7			149	24.0	8	17.0	6	12.2	14	14.6
4	1896	15.5	27	12.1	53	15.3	4	7.8			84	13.5	4	8.5	9	18.4	13	13.5
5	944	7.7	11	4.9	28	8.1	6	11.8			45	7.3	0	0.0	2	4.1	2	2.1
6+	974	7.9	20	9.0	29	8.4	1	2.0			50	8.1	4	8.5	2	4.1	6	6.3
total	12262	100.0	223	100.0	347	100.0	51	100.0			621	100.0	47	100.0	49	100.0	96	100.0
no information	23		4		6		7				17		1		0		1	

two-parents/fatherless by no. of children (1,2,3,4,5,6+)
χ^2 (linear trend) = 2.18 (1df)
χ^2 (departure from trend) = 17.0 (4df)**

two-parents/death of father by no. of children (1,2,3,4,5,6+)
χ^2 (linear trend) = 3.61 (3df)
χ^2 (departure from trend) = 9.97 (4df)*

two-parent/illegitimate by no. of children (1,2,3,4,5+)
χ^2 (linear trend) = 0.95 (3df)
χ^2 (departure from trend) = 15.10 (3df)**

death of father/marital breakdown by no. of children (1,2,3,4,5,6+)
χ^2 (linear trend) = 3.41 (2df)
χ^2 (departure from trend) = 4.03 (4df)

two-parent/motherless by no. of children (1,2,3,4,5+)
χ^2 (linear trend) = 8.82 (1df)**
χ^2 (departure from trend) = 9.80 (3df)*

death of mother/marital breakdown by no. of children (1,2,3,4+)
χ^2 (linear trend) = 1.03 (1df)
χ^2 (departure from trend) = 0.98 (2df)

Table A7.1: Number of children in different family situations receiving Supplementary Benefit in the 12 months before follow-up survey

(a) all social classes

Supplementary Benefit received	two parents		fatherless								motherless					
			death of father		marital breakdown		illegitimate		all fatherless		death of mother		marital breakdown		all motherless	
	N	%	N	%	N	%	N	%	N	%	N	%	N	%	N	%
yes	670	5.6	52	24.9	204	60.9	24	48.0	280	47.1	8	16.7	5	10.2	13	13.4
no	11371	94.4	157	75.1	131	39.1	26	52.0	314	52.9	40	83.3	44	89.8	84	86.6
total	12041	100.0	209	100.0	335	100.0	50	100.0	594	100.0	48	100.0	49	100.0	97	100.0
no information	244		18		18		8		44		0		0		0	

two-parent/motherless by Supplementary Benefit (yes, no) $\chi^2 = 9.70$ (1df) **
fatherless/motherless by Supplementary Benefit (yes, no) $\chi^2 = 37.49$ (1df) ***
two-parent/death of father by Supplementary Benefit (yes, no) $\chi^2 = 134.73$ (1df) ***
illegitimate/marital breakdown by Supplementary Benefit (yes, no) $\chi^2 = 2.49$ (2df)
illegitimate, marital breakdown/death of father by Supplementary Benefit (yes, no) $\chi^2 = 62.74$ (2df) ***

death of mother/marital breakdown by Supplementary Benefit (yes, no) $\chi^2 = 0.40$ (1df)

continued on page 158

Table A7.1: *continued from page 157*

(b) non-manual only

Supplementary Benefit received	two parents		fatherless					
			death of father		marital breakdown		both fatherless	
	N	%	N	%	N	%	N	%
yes	46	1.5	11	19.6	26	39.4	40	31.3
no	3108	98.5	45	80.4	40	60.6	88	68.8
total	3154	100.0	56	100.0	66	100.0	128	100.0
no information	80		2		2		4	

two-parent/fatherless by SB (yes, no)   p = .00 ***   two-parent/death of father by SB (yes, no)   p = .00 ***

death of father/marital breakdown by SB (yes, no) $\chi^2 = 4.70$ (1df) *

(c) manual only

Supplementary Benefit received	two parents		fatherless						motherless					
			death of father		marital breakdown		both fatherless		death of mother		marital breakdown		all motherless	
	N	%	N	%	N	%	N	%	N	%	N	%	N	%
yes	555	6.9	33	25.4	151	68.6	197	52.0	8	21.6	5	14.7	13	18.3
no	7452	93.1	97	74.6	69	31.4	182	48.0	29	78.4	29	85.3	58	81.7
total	8007	100.0	130	100.0	220	100.0	379	100.0	37	100.0	34	100.0	71	100.0
no information	162		13		14		31		0		0		0	

two-parent/death of father by SB (yes, no) $\chi^2 = 62.25$ (1df) ***

death of father/marital breakdown by SB (yes, no) $\chi^2 = 59.59$ (1df) ***

two-parent/motherless by SB (yes, no)   p = .001 ***

death of mother/marital breakdown by SB (yes, no) $\chi^2 = 0.20$ (1df)

Table A7.3 Number of children in different family situations receiving free school meals

(a) all social classes

free meals	two parents		fatherless								death of father		marital breakdown		illegitimate		all fatherless		motherless					
											death of father		marital breakdown		illegitimate		all fatherless		death of mother		marital breakdown		all motherless	
	N	%									N	%	N	%	N	%	N	%	N	%	N	%	N	%
yes	916	7.6									107	48.6	238	68.6	28	53.8	373	60.3	8	16.7	8	16.3	16	16.5
no	11183	92.4									113	51.4	109	31.4	24	46.2	246	39.7	40	83.3	41	83.7	81	83.5
total	12099	100.0									220	100.0	347	100.0	52	100.0	619	100.0	48	100.0	49	100.0	97	100.0
no information	186										7		6		6		19		0		0		0	

two-parent/motherless by free meals (yes, no) $\chi^2 = 9.63$ (1df) ***
fatherless/motherless by free meals (yes, no) $\chi^2 = 62.98$ (1df) ***
death of father/illegitimate by free meals (yes, no) $\chi^2 = 0.27$ (2df)
death of father, illegitimate/marital breakdown by free meals (yes, no) $\chi^2 = 22.09$ (2df) ***

continued on page 160

Table A7.3:*continued from page 159*

(b) non-manual only

free meals	two parents		fatherless				both fatherless	
			death of father		marital breakdown			
	N	%	N	%	N	%	N	%
yes	90	2.8	19	33.9	28	41.2	51	39.2
no	3109	97.2	37	66.1	40	58.8	79	60.8
total	3199	100.0	56	100.0	68	100.0	130	100.0
no information	35		2		0		2	

two-parent/fatherless by free school meals (yes, no) $\chi^2 = 399.53$ (1df) ***
death of father/marital breakdown by free school meals (yes, no) $\chi^2 = 0.41$ (2df)

continued on page 161

Table A7.3: continued from page 160

(c) manual only

free meals	two parents		fatherless						motherless					
			death of father		marital breakdown		both fatherless		death of mother		marital breakdown		all motherless	
	N	%	N	%	N	%	N	%	N	%	N	%	N	%
yes	726	9.1	75	54.0	180	78.6	269	67.6	7	18.9	5	14.7	12	16.9
no	7294	90.9	64	46.0	49	21.4	129	32.4	30	81.1	29	85.3	59	83.1
total	8020	100.0	139	100.0	229	100.0	398	100.0	37	100.0	34	100.0	71	100.0
no information	149		4		5		12		0		0		0	

two-parent/motherless by free school meals (yes, no) $\chi^2 = 4.33$ (1df) *
fatherless/motherless by free school meals (yes, no) $\chi^2 = 62.36$ (1df) ***
death of father/marital breakdown by free school meals (yes, no) $\chi^2 = 23.55$ (2df) ***

Table A8.1: Employment situation of mothers in different family situations during the twelve months before the follow-up survey

(a) All social classes

employment situation	two parents		fatherless							
			death of father		marital breakdown		illegitimate		all fatherless	
	N	%	N	%	N	%	N	%	N	%
full time work only	2264	18.4	74	32.6	100	28.3	25	43.1	199	31.2
part time work only	4384	35.7	72	31.7	98	27.8	9	15.5	179	28.1
full time and part time work	288	2.4	6	2.6	10	2.8	1	1.7	17	2.7
not worked	5343	43.5	75	33.0	145	41.1	23	39.7	243	38.1
total	12279	100.0	227	100.0	353	100.0	58	100.0	638	100.0
No information	6		0		0		0		0	

fatherless/two parent by employed/not employed $\chi^2 = 7.08$ (1df) **
marital breakdown/illegitimate by employed/not employed $\chi^2 = 0.00$ (2df)
marital breakdown, illegitimate/two parents by employed/not employed $\chi^2 = 1.02$ (1df)
marital breakdown, illegitimate/death of father by employed/not employed $\chi^2 = 3.48$ (2df)

fatherless/two parent by full/part time only $\chi^2 = 53.48$ (1df) ***
death of father, marital breakdown/illegitimate by employed/not employed $\chi^2 = 5.65$ (2df)

continued on page 163

Table A8.1: *continued from page 162*

(b) non-manual only

employment situation	two parents		death of father		marital breakdown		both fatherless	
	N	%	N	%	N	%	N	%
full time work only	494	15.3	16	27.6	20	29.4	36	28.6
part time work only	1024	31.7	18	31.0	21	30.9	39	31.0
full time and part time work	65	2.0	3	5.2	2	2.9	5	4.0
not worked	1646	51.0	21	36.2	25	36.8	46	36.5
total	3229	100.0	58	100.0	68	100.0	126	100.0
no information	5		0		0		0	

fatherless/two parent by employed/not employed χ^2 = 9.58 (1df) **
fatherless/two parent by full/part time only χ^2 = 7.01 (1df) **

(c) manual only

employment situation	two parents		death of father		marital breakdown		both fatherless	
	N	%	N	%	N	%	N	%
full work only	1580	19.4	50	35.0	59	25.3	109	29.0
part time work only	3109	38.1	49	34.3	72	30.9	121	32.2
full time and part time work	198	2.4	3	2.1	6	2.6	9	2.4
not worked	3265	40.1	41	28.7	96	41.2	137	36.4
total	8152	100.0	143	100.0	233	100.0	376	100.0
no information	17		0		1		1	

fatherless/two parent by employed/not employed χ^2 = 1.81 (1df)
marital breakdown/two parent by employed/not employed χ^2 = 0.08 (1df)
fatherless/two parent by full/part time only χ^2 = 17.64 (1df) ***
death of father/marital breakdown by full/part time only χ^2 = 0.47 (1df)

Table A8.6: Number of weeks fathers were off work through unemployment in the twelve months before the follow-up survey.

(a) all social classes

weeks off work through unemployment	two parents		death of mother		marital breakdown		all motherless	
	N	%	N	%	N	%	N	%
none	10205	92.5	39	83.0	40	83.3	79	83.2
1—4	222	2.0	2	4.3	1	2.1	3	3.2
5—13	280	2.5	0	0.0	3	6.3	3	3.2
14—26	149	1.4	1	2.1	1	2.1	2	2.1
27+	171	1.6	5	10.6	3	6.3	8	8.4
total	11027	100.0	47	100.0	48	100.0	95	100.0
no information	1258		1		1		2	

motherless/two parents by unemployed, yes/no χ^2 = 10.61 (1df) **
death of mother/marital breakdown by unemployed, yes/no χ^2 = 0.05 (1df)

(b) manual only

weeks off work through unemployment	two parents		all motherless	
	N	%	N	%
none	6296	90.4	57	82.6
1—4	181	2.6	2	2.9
5—13	224	3.2	2	2.9
14—26	122	1.8	2	2.9
27+	143	2.1	6	8.7
total	6966	100.0	69	100.0
no information	766		1	

motherless/two parents by unemployed, yes/no χ^2 = 3.87 (1df) *

Table A9.2 Tenure of accommodation occupied by children in different family situations at eleven

a) all social classes

tenure	two parents		death of father		fatherless marital breakdown		illegitimate		all fatherless		death of mother		motherless marital breakdown		all motherless	
	N	%	N	%	N	%	N	%	N	%	N	%	N	%	N	%
owned	5814	49.9	83	38.2	63	18.8	6	12.0	152	25.2	15	33.3	18	38.3	33	35.9
council-rented	4993	42.9	115	53.0	205	61.0	31	62.0	351	58.2	24	53.3	25	53.2	49	53.3
private-rented (unfurnished)	772	6.6	19	8.8	53	15.8	5	10.0	77	12.8	6	13.3	2	4.3	8	8.7
private-rented (furnished)	63	0.5	0	0.0	15	4.5	8	16.0	23	3.8	0	0.0	2	4.3	2	2.2
total	11642	100.0	217	100.0	336	100.0	50	100.0	603	100.0	45	100.0	47	100.0	92	100.0
other or no information	643		10		17		8		35		3		2		5	

notes for this table are on page 166

Table A9.2:continued from page 165

two-parent/fatherless by owned/rented	χ^2 = 139.38 (1df)***
two-parent/death of father by owned/rented	χ^2 = 11.18 (1df)***
marital breakdown/illegitimate by owned/rented	χ^2 = 0.93 (2df)
death of father/marital breakdown,	
illeg. by owned/rented	χ^2 = 29.51 (2df)***
two-parent/motherless by owned/rented	χ^2 = 6.68 (1df)**
death of mother/marital breakdown,	
by owner/rented	χ^2 = 0.08 (1df)
motherless/fatherless by owner/rented	χ^2 = 4.12 (1df)*
two-parent/fatherless by privately rented/other	χ^2 = 70.67 (1df)***
two-parent/death of father by privately rented/other	χ^2 = 0.58 (1df)
marital breakdown/illeg. by privately rented/other	χ^2 = 0.56 (2df)
marital breakdown, illeg./death of father by	
privately rented/other	χ^2 = 14.15 (2df)***
two-parent/motherless by privately rented/other	χ^2 = 1.35 (1df)
death of mother/marital breakdown by	
privately rented/other	P = 0.34 (1df)
fatherless/motherless by privately rented/other	χ^2 = 1.55 (1df)

b) manual only

	two-parents		motherless					
			death of mother		*marital breakdown*		*all motherless*	
tenure:	N	%	N	%	N	%	N	%
owned	2958	38.3	11	32.4	11	33.3	22	32.8
council rented	4203	54.4	20	58.8	20	60.6	40	59.7
privately rented (unfurnished)	544	7.0	3	8.8	1	3.0	4	6.0
privately rented (furnished)	27	0.3	0	0.0	1	3.0	1	1.5
total	7732	100.0	34	100.0	33	100.0	67	100.0
no information	437		3		1		4	

two-parent/motherless by owned/rented	χ^2 = 0.61 (1df)

Table A9.4: Use of basic household amenities by children in different family situations at eleven

use of amenities	two parents		fatherless								motherless					
			death of father		marital breakdown		illegitimate		all fatherless		death of mother		marital breakdown		all motherless	
	N	%	N	%	N	%	N	%	N	%	N	%	N	%	N	%
sole use of all 3	10733	87.4	188	84.3	245	70.6	34	65.4	467	75.1	35	72.9	43	87.8	78	80.4
shared or no use of at least one	1545	12.6	35	15.7	102	29.4	18	34.6	155	24.9	13	27.1	6	12.2	19	19.6
total	12278	100.0	223	100.0	347	100.0	52	100.0	622	100.0	48	100.0	49	100.0	97	100.0
no information	7		4		6		6		16		0		0		0	

two-parent/fatherless by sole use of all 3 (yes, no) $\chi^2 = 77.67$ (1df) ***

two-parent/death of father by sole use of all 3 (yes, no) $\chi^2 = 1.65$ (1df)

marital breakdown/illegitimate by sole use of all 3 (yes, no) $\chi^2 = 0.36$ (2df)

marital breakdown, illeg./death of father by sole use of all 3 (yes, no) $\chi^2 = 15.05$ (2df) ***

two-parent/motherless by sole use of all 3 (yes, no) $\chi^2 = 3.67$ (1df)

death of mother/marital breakdown by sole use of all 3 (yes, no) $\chi^2 = 2.51$ (1 df)

Table A9.12: Number of moves since birth made by children in different family situations at eleven

number of moves	two-parents		fatherless								motherless					
			death of father		marital breakdown		illegitimate		all fatherless		death of mother		marital breakdown		all motherless	
	N	%	N	%	N	%	N	%	N	%	N	%	N	%	N	%
0	3317	25.7	82	37.3	49	14.2	14	27.5	145	23.6	18	39.1	13	27.1	31	33.0
1	4460	36.7	74	33.6	80	23.3	11	21.6	165	26.8	13	28.3	15	31.3	28	29.8
2	2121	17.5	28	12.7	72	20.9	5	9.8	105	17.1	8	17.4	7	14.6	15	16.0
3	1165	9.6	20	9.1	57	16.6	7	13.7	84	13.7	5	10.9	6	12.5	11	11.7
4	567	4.7	4	1.8	25	7.3	4	7.8	33	5.4	2	4.3	2	4.2	4	4.3
5+	708	5.8	12	5.5	61	17.7	10	19.6	83	13.5	0	0.0	5	10.4	5	5.3
total	12138	100.0	220	100.0	344	100.0	51	100.0	615	100.0	46	100.0	48	100.0	94	100.0
no information	147		7		9		7		23		2		1		3	

two-parent/death of father by no. of moves (0,1,2,3,4,5+) χ^2 (linear trend) = 9.52 (1df) **
                                                            χ^2 (departure from trend) = 10.54 (4df) *

two-parent/marital breakdown by no. of moves (0,1,2,3,4,5+) χ^2 (linear trend) = 66.55 (1df) ***
                                                            χ^2 (departure from trend) = 12.65 (4df)*

two-parent/illegitimate by no. of moves (0,1,2,3,4+) χ^2 (linear trend) = 1.40 (1df)
                                                       χ^2 (departure from trend) = 9.93 (3df) *

two-parent/motherless by no. of moves (0,1,2,3,4+) χ^2 (linear trend) = 0.16 (1df)
                                                     χ^2 (departure from trend) = 3.30 (3df)

death of mother/marital breakdown by no. of moves (0,1,2,3+) χ^2 (linear trend) = 2.17 (1df)
                                                               χ^2 (departure from trend) = 0.78 (2df)

Table A10.1: Number of contacts made with social and/or welfare agencies by families in different parental situations since study child's 7th birthday.

| number of contacts | two-parents | | fatherless | | | | | | | | | motherless | | | | | |
| | | | death of father | | marital breakdown | | illegitimate | | all fatherless | | | death of mother | | marital breakdown | | all motherless | |
	N	%	N	%	N	%	N	%	N	%		N	%	N	%	N	%
0	11,325	92.2	177	78.0	201	56.9	37	63.8	415	65.1		39	81.3	28	57.1	67	69.1
1	701	5.7	39	17.2	97	27.5	10	17.2	146	22.9		5	10.4	16	32.7	21	21.7
2	178	1.5	8	3.5	39	11.1	5	8.6	52	8.1		3	6.2	4	8.2	7	7.2
3	55	0.5	3	1.3	10	2.8	5	8.6	18	2.8		1	2.1	0	0.0	1	1.0
4+	26	0.2	0	0.0	6	1.7	1	1.7	7	1.1		0	0.0	1	2.0	1	1.0
total	12,285	100.0	227	100.0	353	100.0	58	100.0	638	100.0		48	100.0	49	100.0	97	100.0

two-parent/fatherless by no. of agencies contacted (0,1,2,3,4+)

χ^2 (linear trend) = 158.34 (1df) ***
χ^2 (departure from trend) = 20.69 (3df) ***

two-parent/death of father by no. of agencies contacted (0,1,2+)

χ^2 (linear trend) = 18.56 (1df) ***

marital breakdown/illegitimate by no. of agencies contacted (0,1,2,3+)

χ^2 (departure from trend) = 5.84 (1df) *
χ^2 (linear trend) = 0.15 (2df)

death of father/marital breakdown, illegitimate by no. of agencies contacted (0,1,2+)

χ^2 (departure from trend) = 5.06 (7df)

two parent/motherless by no. of agencies contacted (0,1,2+)

χ^2 (linear trend) = 40.61 (2df) ***
χ^2 (departure from trend) = 0.16 (7df)

death of mother/marital breakdown by no. of agencies contacted (0,1,2+)

χ^2 (linear trend) = 18.50 (1df) ***
χ^2 (departure from trend) = 1.26 (1df) *
χ^2 (linear trend) = 5.07 (1df) *
χ^2 (departure from trend) = 4.62 (1df) *

Table A10.3: Number of children in different family situations at 11 who had been in care at some time since birth

in care	two-parents		fatherless								motherless					
---	---	---	death of father		marital breakdown		illegitimate		all fatherless		death of mother		marital breakdown		all motherless	
	N	%	N	%	N	%	N	%	N	%	N	%	N	%	N	%
local auth. only	201	1.7	8	3.6	31	9.0	10	20.0	49	8.0	3	6.3	6	12.2	9	9.3
voluntary society only	17	0.1	0	0.0	9	2.6	2	4.0	11	1.8	1	2.1	1	2.0	2	2.1
both local authority & voluntary society	17	0.1	0	0.0	0	0.0	0	0.0	0	0.0	0	0.0	1	2.0	1	1.0
never in care	11,894	98.1	212	96.4	304	88.4	38	76.0	554	90.2	44	91.7	41	83.7	85	87.6
total	12,129	100.0	220	100.0	344	100.0	50	100.0	614	100.0	48	100.0	49	100.0	97	100.0
no information	156		7		9		8		24		0		0		0	

two parent/fatherless by in care (yes, no) $\chi^2 = 155.18$ (1df) ***
two parent/death of father by in care (yes, no)   p = 0.14
two parent/motherless by in care (yes, no)   p = 0.00 ***

Table A12.4: Analysis of reading score (1)

Dependent variable is score on reading comprehension test at 11
Independent variables are shown below
Sample size = 10457   Overall sample mean = 15.97

Fitted constants and analysis of variance table
Significance levels are those obtained after fitting all other main effects.

Source	simple deviations from overall sample mean	fitted constants	MS ratio	DF	Significance level
parental situation:					
two parents	1.22	0.52	1.25	4	NS
fatherless: father dead	0.97	0.65			
fatherless: marital breakdown	−1.08	0.01			
motherless: mother dead	−0.63	−0.46			
motherless: marital breakdown	−0.48	−0.72			
Social class					
1 & 2		2.57	145.4	4	***
3 non-manual		0.79			
3 manual		−0.55			
4		−1.01			
5		−1.81			
Sex					
boy		−0.07	1.79	1	NS
girl		0.07			
free school meals					
yes		−0.74	47.49	1	***
no		0.74			
ever in care					
yes		−0.72	13.47	1	***
no		0.72			
amenities					
Sole use of all		0.57	43.90	1	***
other		−0.57			
no. of children					
1		1.64	93.32	4	***
2		1.02			
3		−0.02			
4		−0.75			
5+		−1.89			
no. of schools					
1,2		0.25	10.43	1	***
3+		−0.25			
parental aspirations:					
stay on at school		1.67	651.8	1	***
other		−1.67			
overall constant		12.90			

Table A12.7 Analysis of reading score (2)

Dependent variable is score on reading comprehension test at 11
Independent variables are shown below
Sample size = 10175

Fitted constants and analysis of variance table
Significance levels are those obtained after fitting all other main effects.

Source	simple deviations from overall sample mean	fitted constants	F ratio	DF	Significance level
parental situation:/social class					
two parents non-manual	3.15	1.12	38.23	6	***
two parents manual	−0.68	−0.82			
fatherless: father dead non-manual	3.64	2.02			
fatherless: father dead manual	−1.18	−0.81			
fatherless: marital breakdown n-m	1.46	0.90			
fatherless: marital breakdown m.	−3.09	−1.52			
fatherless: illegitimate	−1.68	−0.89			
Mother working					
full time		−0.37	8.49	2	***
part time		0.11			
not at all		0.26			
Sex					
boy		−0.07	1.81	1	NS
girl		0.07			
free school meals					
yes		−0.75	48.11	1	***
no		0.75			
ever in care					
yes		−0.77	15.62	1	***
no		0.77			
amenities					
sole use of all		0.55	40.56	1	***
other		−0.55			
no. of children					
1		1.79	100.6	4	***
2		1.03			
3		−0.06			
4		−0.79			
5+		−1.97			
no. of schools					
1,2		0.26	10.86	1	***
3+		−0.26			
mother stayed at school					
yes		1.13	288.6	1	***
no		−1.13			
parental aspirations:					
stay on at school		1.59	578.7	1	***
other		−1.59			
overall constant		14.6			

*F ratio when all other effects fitted (not interaction)

Table A 12.8: Analysis of reading score (2). Fitted constants for parental situation/social class × mother working (calculated from main effects and interaction)

Parental situation	full-time	part-time	not working
two parents: non-manual	0.92	1.44	1.58
two parents: manual	-1.03	-0.51	-0.37
fatherless: father dead: non-manual	2.49	2.03	2.17
fatherless: father dead: manual	-0.42	-0.88	-0.74
fatherless: marital breakdown: non-manual	0.69	1.19	1.33
fatherless: marital breakdown: manual	-1.73	-1.23	-1.09
fatherless: Illegitimate	1.45	-2.87	-2.73

test for interaction: F ratio = 7.27   df=12   Sig. level = ***

Table 12.9: Mean reading scores at 11 of boys and girls in different family situations

(no. of children in brackets)

family situation		boys		girls		total
two parents		16.21	(5822)	16.26	(5565)	16.23	(11447)
fatherless:	father dead	15.07	(110)	16.22	(99)	15.62	(209)
	marital breakdown	13.88	(144)	14.15	(184)	14.03	(328)
	illegitimate	12.92	(26)	13.14	(28)	13.04	(54)
	all fatherless	14.26	(280)	14.72	(311)	14.50	(591)
motherless:	mother dead	14.21	(24)	14.48	(23)	14.30	(47)
	marital breakdown	16.23	(26)	12.56	(16)	14.83	(42)
	all motherless	15.26	(50)	13.69	(39)	14.57	(89)

Table A12.10 Analysis of arithmetic score (1)

Dependent variable is score on the arithmetic test at 11
Independent variables are as shown below
Sample size = 10454   Overall sample mean = 16.62

Fitted constant and analysis of variance table
Significance levels are those obtained after fitting all other main effects

Source	simple deviations from overall sample mean	fitted constants	MS ratio	DF	Significance level
parental situation:					
two parents	2.56	1.23	3.40	4	**
fatherless: father dead	1.76	1.17			
fatherless: marital breakdown	−2.17	−0.69			
motherless: mother dead	−0.73	−0.02			
motherless: marital breakdown	−1.42	−1.69			
Social class					
1 & 2		4.65	167.60	4	***
3 non-manual		1.36			
3 manual		−0.95			
4		−1.62			
5		−3.44			
Sex					
boy		0.14	2.45	1	NS
girl		−0.14			
free school meals					
yes		−1.01	30.99	1	***
no		1.01			
ever in care					
yes		−1.54	22.23	1	***
no		1.54			
amenities					
Sole use of all		0.92	40.59	1	***
other		−0.92			
no. of children					
1		0.63	38.24	4	***
2		1.59			
3		0.27			
4		−0.54			
5+		−1.95			
no. of schools					
1,2		0.39	8.70	1	**
3+		−0.39			
parental aspirations:					
stay on at school		2.92	709.80	1	***
other		−2.92			
overall constant		10.94			

Appendix 2

Table 12.12: Mean Arithmetic scores at 11 of boys and girls in different family situations

(no. of children in brackets)

family situation	boys		girls		total	
two parents	17.39	(5881)	16.92	(5563)	17.16	(11444)
fatherless:						
father dead	15.07	(110)	16.75	(99)	15.87	(209)
marital breakdown	13.13	(144)	12.45	(184)	12.75	(328)
illegitimate	12.58	(26)	12.07	(28)	12.31	(54)
all fatherless	13.84	(280)	13.78	(311)	13.81	(591)
motherless:						
mother dead	13.25	(24)	14.78	(23)	14.00	(47)
marital breakdown	15.54	(26)	11.19	(16)	13.88	(42)
all motherless	14.44	(50)	13.31	(39)	13.94	(89)

Table A12.13: Analysis of arithmetic Score (2)

Dependent variable is score on arithmetic test at 11.
Independent variables are as shown below
Sample size = 10172

Fitted constants and analysis of variance table
Significance levels are those obtained when all other main effects are fitted.

Source	Simple deviations from overall sample mean	Fitted constants	F ratio*	DF	significance level
parental situation:					
two parents, non-manual	5.51	2.42	45.06	6	***
two parents, manual	−1.08	−1.16			
fatherless:					
father dead, non manual	5.81	3.45			
father dead, manual	−2.17	−1.23			
marital breakdown,					
non-manual	0.54	−0.15			
manual	−5.24	−2.65			
illegitimate	−1.08	−0.68			
mother working:					
full time		−0.44	4.95	2	**
part-time		0.08			
not at all		0.36			
sex:					
boy		0.14	2.35	1	NS
girl					
free school meals:					
yes		−1.10	36.15	1	***
no		1.10			
ever in care:					
yes		−1.66	25.70	1	***
no		1.66			
amenities:					
sole use of all		0.93	41.44	1	***
other		−0.93			

continued on page 177

Table A12.13: *continued from page 166*

---

no of children:
1.	0.88	40.29	4	***
2.	1.58			
3.	0.20			
4.	−0.59			
5+	−2.07			

---

no. of schools:
1, 2	0.41	9.48	1	**
3+	−0.41			

---

mother stayed at school:
yes	1.92	293.70	1	***
no	−1.92			

---

parental aspirations:
stay on at school	2.79	636.50	1	***
other	−2.79			

---

overall constant   13.03

*F ratio when all other main effects fitted (not interaction).

Table A12.14: **Analysis of arithmetic (2)**

Fitted constants for parental situation/social class x mother working
(calculated from main effects and interaction)

parental situation	*full-time*	*part-time*	*total*
two parents: non-manual	2.10	2.75	3.02
two parents: manual	−1.48	−0.83	−0.56
fatherless: father dead: non-manual	5.50	2.75	3.02
fatherless: father dead: manual	0.55	−2.20	−1.93
fatherless: marital breakdown: non-manual	−0.27	0.08	0.35
fatherless: marital breakdown: manual	−2.80	−2.45	−2.18
fatherless: illegitimate	1.87	−2.98	−2.71

test for interaction   F ratio = 6.20   df = 12   sig. level ***

Table A12.15: Longitudinal analysis of reading

Dependent variable is score on reading comprehension test at 11
Independent variables are shown below

1. Sample size = 10249

Source	simple deviations from overall sample mean	fitted constants	MS ratio	DF	Significance level
reading score at 7		0.41	6094	1	***
parental situation:					
two parents	0.40	0.35	3.47	2	*
fatherless: father dead	−0.13	0.06			
fatherless: marital breakdown	− 1.76	−0.41			
Social class					
1 & 2		2.02	120.2	4	***
3 non-manual		0.56			
3 manual		−0.36			
4		−0.85			
5		−1.37			
Sex					
boy		0.47	103.3	1	***
girl		−0.47			
overall constant		5.30			

2. Sample size = 9899

Source	simple deviations from overall sample mean	fitted constants	MS ratio	DF	Significance level
reading score at 7		0.41	5938	1	***
parental situation: two parents	0.40	0.35	0.49	2	NS
motherless: mother dead	−1.34	0.00			
motherless: marital breakdown	−1.24	−0.35			
Social class					
1 & 2		2.00	113.8	4	***
3 non-manual		0.55			
3 manual		−0.35			
4		−0.81			
·5		−1.39			
Sex					
boy		0.49	107.4	1	***
girl		−0.49			
Overall constant		5.24			

Table A12.16: Longitudinal analysis of arithmetic

Dependent variable is score on arithmetic test at 11
Independent variables are as shown below.

1. Sample size = 10254

Source	Simple deviations from overall sample mean	Fitted constants	MS ratio	DF	significance level
arithmetic score at 7		2.18	4243	1	•••
parental situation:					
two parents	0.79	1.22	15.46	2	•••
fatherless, father dead	−0.36	0.41			
fatherless					
marital breakdown	−3.80	−1.63			
social class					
1 & 2		4.47	207.6	4	•••
3 non-manual		1.56			
3 manual		−0.72			
4		−1.64			
5		−3.67			
sex					
boy		−0.09	1.19	1	NS
girl		0.09			
overall constant		4.72			

2. Sample size = 9905

Source	Simple deviations	Fitted constants	MS ratio	DF	significance level
arithmetic score at 7		2.19	4137	1	•••
parental situation:					
two-parents	0.79	1.03	1.28	2	NS
motherless, mother dead	−2.40	−0.37			
motherless,					
marital breakdown	−2.20	−0.66			
social class:					
1 & 2		4.47	200.2	4	•••
3 non-manual		1.55			
3 manual		−0.74			
4		−1.56			
5		−3.72			
sex					
boy		−0.06	−0.46	1	NS
girl		0.06			
overall constant		4.87			

Table A13.1: Analysis of social adjustment

Dependent variable is Bristol Social Adjustment Guide Score
Independent variables are as shown below.
Sample size = 10379   Overall sample mean = 8.33

Fitted constants and analysis of variance table
Significance levels are those obtained after fitting all other main effects

Source	simple deviations from overall sample mean	fitted constants	MS ratio	DF	Significance level
parental situation:					
two parents	−0.42	−0.24	0.95	4	NS
fatherless: father dead	−0.56	−0.81			
fatherless: marital breakdown	2.01	0.58			
motherless: mother dead	0.45	−0.40			
motherless: marital breakdown	1.81	0.87			
Social class					
1 & 2		−1.19	17.84	4	***
3 non-manual		−0.81			
3 manual		0.10			
4		0.59			
5		1.31			
free school meals					
yes		0.72	19.66	1	***
no		−0.72			
ever in care					
yes		1.44	23.76	1	***
no		−1.44			
amenities					
sole use of all		−0.52	16.14	1	***
other		0.52			
no. of children					
1		−0.63	21.14	4	***
2		−0.85			
3		−0.43			
4		0.43			
5+		1.48			
no. of schools					
1,2		−0.57	22.48	1	***
3+		0.57			
parental aspirations:					
stay on at school		−1.45	215.5	1	***
other		1.45			
Sex					
boy		1.38	286.3	1	***
girl		−1.38			
overall constant		11.95			

Table A13.2: Mean scores on the Bristol Social Adjustment Guide of boys and girls in different family situations at 11.

family situation	boys		girls		total	
			(number of children in brackets)			
two parents	9.43	(5880)	6.68	(5558)	8.09	(11438)
fatherless:						
father dead	9.02	(110)	7.25	(99)	8.18	(209)
marital breakdown	13.03	(145)	8.35	(187)	10.39	(332)
illegitimate	14.00	(27)	9.33	(27)	11.67	(54)
all fatherless	11.56	(282)	8.09	(313)	9.73	(595)
motherless:						
mother dead	11.46	(24)	7.17	(23)	9.36	(47)
marital breakdown	10.32	(28)	8.65	(17)	9.69	(45)
all motherless	10.85	(52)	7.80	(4)	9.52	(92)

Table A 13.5: Analysis of social adjustment (2)

Dependent variable is Bristol Social Adjustment Guide Score
Independent variable are as shown below
Sample size = 10098

Fitted constants and analysis of variance table

Significance levels are those obtained after fitting all other main effects.

Source	Simple deviation from overall sample mean	Fitted constants	M.S. ratio	DF	significance level
parental situation/social class:					
two parents non-manual	−2.11	−0.51	4.08	6	***
tow parents manual	0.21	0.42			
fatherless					
father dead non-manual	−1.37	−0.36			
father dead manual	−0.26	−0.69			
marital breakdown					
non-manual	1.00	1.18			
marital breakdown manual	2.32	0.70			
illegitimate	0.72	−0.74			
mother worked:					
full-time		0.46	5.45	2	**
part-time		−0.18			
not at all		−0.28			
sex:					
boy		1.36	274.1	1	***
girl		−1.36			
free school meals:					
yes		0.84	25.6	1	***
no		−0.84			
ever in care:					
yes		1.56	27.4	1	***
no		−1.56			
amenities:					
sole use of all		−0.55	17.6	1	***
other		0.55			

continued on page 183

Table A13.5: *continued from page 182*

no of children				
1	−0.79	23.1	4	***
2	−0.89			
3	−0.38			
4	0.52			
5+	1.54			
no of schools:				
1,2	−0.55	20.5	1	***
3+	0.55			
mother stayed on at school:				
yes	−0.55	29.7	1	***
no	0.55			
parental aspirations:				
stay on at school	−1.42	200.1	1	***
other	1.42			
overall constant	11.52			

List of Supplementary tables available from the British Library

---

S5.6   Number of children in fatherless families due to death or marital breakdown i) at 7; ii) at 11.

S5.7   Number of boys and girls in fatherless and motherless families at eleven, by cause of situation.

S5.8   Care situation at eleven of children in fatherless families at seven, by cause of breakdown.

S5.9   Care situation at eleven of children who had lost own mother and stayed with own father.

S6.1   Social class background of children living with or without both natural parents at 11.

S6.3   Size of family among children in different family situations at 11: (b) non-manual only (c) manual only.

S6.4   Number of 11-year old children in different family situations with siblings living away from home.

S6.5   Age of mothers in fatherless and two-parent families when study child was 11.

S6.6   Age of fathers in motherless and two-parent families when study child was eleven.

S7.2   Number of children in families with Supplementary Benefit as sole source of income in the 12 months before follow-up survey.

S7.4   Perceived financial hardship among families with children receiving free school meals.

S8.2   Number of mothers in employment during the twelve months prior to the follow-up by the number of children in the family.

S8.3   Number of mothers who stayed at school after the minimum leaving age.

S8.4   Most recent job held by mothers in different family situations when study child aged 11: a) mothers who stayed on at school; b) mothers who left school at minimum leaving age.

S8.5   Hours spent away from home outside 9.a.m. to 4.00. p.m. by mothers in different family situations.

S9.1   Type of accommodation occupied by children in different family situations at 11.

S9.3   Tenure of accommodation among 11-year-old children who were in owner-occupied accommodation at seven.

S9.5   Use of basic household amenities at 11 among children who had sole use of all three at seven.

S9.6   Use of basic household amenities by children in privately rented accommodation at eleven.

S9.7   Use of basic household amenities by children in local authority accommodation at eleven.

S9.8   Number of children in different family situations living in crowded homes at eleven.

S9.9   Number of children living in privately rented accommodation who were crowded at eleven.

S9.10   Number of children in different family situations who were sharing a bed at eleven.

S9.11   Number of children in privately rented accommodation who were sharing a bed at eleven.

S9.13   Number of moves since birth made by children in privately rented accommodation at eleven.

S9.14   Number of schools attended by children in different family situations at eleven.

S9.15   Level of satisfaction with accommodation in different family situations.

S9.16   Level of satisfaction among tenants of privately rented accommodation.

S10.2   Number of families who had had contact with each separate department or organization.

S11.1   Discussion initiated with school staff by parents in different family situations.

S11.2   Teachers' ratings of interest shown by mothers in different family situations.

S11.3   Teachers' ratings of interest shown by mothers in different family situations who had visited their children's school.

S11.4   Teachers' ratings of interest shown by fathers in different family situations.

S11.5   School leaving age chosen for boys by parents in different family situations.

S11.6   School leaving age chosen for girls by parents in different family situations.

S11.7   Aspirations of parents in different family situations for boys' further education.

S11.8   Aspirations of parents in different family situations for girls' further education.

S11.9   Frequency of outings with mother among children in different family situations.

S11.10   Frequency of outings with mother in different family and work situations.

S11.11   Frequency of outings with father among children in different family situations.

S12.1   Number of children in different family situations attending special schools at the age of eleven.

S12.2   Number of children in different family situations considered likely to benefit from special schooling.

S12.3   Number of children in different family situations receiving help in school for backwardness.

S12.5   Analysis of reading score (1): fitted constants after allowing for all main effects except free school meals.

S12.6   Mean reading scores at 11 of children in different family situations, by receipt of free school meals.

S12.11   Mean arithmetic scores at 11 by children in different family situations, by receipt of free school meals.

S12.17   Longitudinal analysis of arithmetic. Fitted constants for sex X parental situation.

S13.3   Analysis of social adjustment (1): Fitted constants after allowing for all main effects except free school meals.

S13.4   Mean scores on the BSAG at 11 of children in different family situations, by receipt of free school meals.

S13.6   Mean scores of BSAG at 11 of children in different family situations, by mothers' employment situation.

S13.7   (a) Parents' ratings of boys' behaviour.
         (b) Parents' ratings of girls' behaviour.

S13.8   Parents' ratings of children's developmental difficulties.

S13.9   Prevalance of nocturnal enuresis among children in different family situations at eleven.

S13.10   Prevalence of nocturnal enuresis at eleven among children in different family situations who were wet at night between five and seven.

S13.11   Prevalence of nocturnal enuresis between five and seven of children in different family situations who were wet at night at eleven.

S13.12   Prevalence of nocturnal enuresis at eleven among children in different family situations who were dry at night between five and seven.

S14.1   Boys' intentions regarding further study or employment after leaving school.

Bibliography

ANDRY, R.G. (1962) 'Paternal and maternal roles in delinquency.' In: AINSWORTH, M.D. *et al. Deprivation of Maternal Care*. Geneva: World Health Organisation.

ANDRY, R.G. (1971) *Delinquency and Parental Pathology*. rev. ed. London: Staples Press.

BAPKAR, V.P. (1968) 'On the analysis of contingency tables with a quantitative response,' *Biometrics*, **24**, 329–38.

BARCLAY, A. and SUSUMANO, D.R. (1967) 'Father absence, cross-sex identity and field-dependent behaviour in male adolescents', *Child Development*, **38** 1, 243–50.

BARKER LUNN, J.C. (1970) *Streaming in the Primary School*. Slough: NFER.

BARTLETT, C.J. and HORROCKS, J.E. (1968) 'A study of the needs status of adolescents from broken homes,' *Journal of Genetic Psychology*, **43**, 153–9.

BELL, N.W. and VOGEL, E.F. (Eds.) (1968) *A Modern Introduction to the Family*. rev. ed. New York: Free Press.

BILLER, H.B. (1968) 'A note on father absence and masculine development in lower-class negro and white boys,' *Child Development*, **39**, 3, 1003–6.

BILLER, H.B. (1969) 'Father absence, maternal encouragement, and sex role development in kindergarten-age boys,' *Child Development*, **40**, 2, 539–46.

BLAKE, P. (1972) *The Plight of One-Parent Families*. London: Council for Children's Welfare.

BOTT, E. (1957) *Family and Social Network*. London: Tavistock.

BOWLBY, J. (1966) *Maternal Care and Mental Health*. repr. New York: Schocken Books.

BRONFENBRENNER, U. (1961) 'The changing American child: a speculative analysis,' *Journal of Social Issues*, **17**, 1, 6–18.

BRONFENBRENNER, U. (1970) *Two Worlds of Childhood: US and USSR*. New York: Russell Sage Foundation.

BURCHINALL, L.G. (1964) 'Characteristics of adolescents from unbroken, broken and reconstituted families,' *Journal of Marriage and the Family*, **26**, 44–52.

BURTON, R.V. and WHITING, J.W.M. (1961) 'The absent father and cross-sex identity,' *Merrill-Palmer Quarterly*, **7**, 85–94.

BUTLER, N.R. and BONHAM, D.G. (1963) *Perinatal Mortality*. Edinburgh: Livingstone.

BUTLER, N.R. and ALBERMAN, E.D. *(Eds.)* (1969) *Perinatal Problems*. Edinburgh: Livingstone.

CARLIER MACKIEWICZ, N. (1969) *Les Veuves et Leurs Familles dans la Societe d'aujourd'hui.* Paris: Caisse Nationale des Allocations Familiales.

CARLSMITH, L. (1964) 'Effects of early father absence on scholastic aptitude,' *Harvard Educational Review,* **34** 1, 1—21.

CATHOLIC HOUSING AID SOCIETY (1972) *Evidence to the Finer Committee on One-Parent Families.* London: Catholic Housing Aid Society.

CENTRAL ADVISORY COUNCIL FOR EDUCATION. (1967) *Children and their Primary Schools.* London: HMSO. 2 vols. (The Plowden report)

CHRISTENSEN, H.T. (ed.) (1964) *Handbook of Marriage and the Family.* Chicago: Rand McNally.

COMFORT, A. (1970) 'Chairman's closing remarks.' In: ELLIOTT, K. *(ed.) The Family and its Future: a Ciba Foundation Symposium.* London: Churchill.

CRELLIN, E., PRINGLE, M.L. Kellmer, and WEST, P. (1971) *Born Illegitimate.* Slough: NFER (A National Children's Bureau report.)

DAGER, E.Z. (1964) 'Socialization and personality development in the child.' In: CHRISTENSEN, H.T. (ed.) *Handbook of Marriage and the Family.* Chicago: Rand McNally.

DAVIE, R., BUTLER, N.R., and GOLDSTEIN, H. (1972) *From Birth to Seven.* London: Longman in assoc with National Children's Bureau.

DEPARTMENT OF HEALTH AND SOCIAL SECURITY (1972) *Families Receiving Supplementary Benefit.* London: HMSO.

DEPARTMENT OF HEALTH AND SOCIAL SECURITY (1974) Report of the Committee on One-Parent Families. London: HMSO. 2 vols. (The Finer report)

DEPARTMENT OF THE ENVIRONMENT (1971) *Report of the Committee on the Rents Act.* London: HMSO. (Francis report.)

DESPERT, J.L. (1962) *Children of Divorce.* New York: Doubleday.

DEUTSCH, M. and BROWN, B. (1964) 'Social influences in negro-white intelligence differences,' *Journal of Social Issues,* **20,** 2, 24—35.

DOUGLAS, J.W.B. (1964) *The Home and the School.* London: MacGibbon and Kee.

DOUGLAS, J.W.B. (1970) 'Broken families and child behaviour,' *Journal of Royal College of Physicians,* **4,** 3, 203—10.

DOUGLAS, J.W.B. and BLOMFIELD, J.M. (1958) *Children under Five.* London: Allen and Unwin.

DOUGLAS, J.W.B., ROSS, J.M. and SIMPSON, H.R. (1968) *All our Future.* London: Peter Davies.

DUNCAN, B. and DUNCAN, O.D. (1969) 'Family stability and occupational success,' *Social Problems,* **16,** 3, 273—85.

EDWARDS, H. and THOMPSON, B. (1971) 'Who are the fatherless?' *New Society*, **17**, 436, 192–3.

FERRI, E. and ROBINSON,H. (1976) *Coping Alone*. Slough: NFER.

FLETCHER, R. (1966) *The Family and Marriage in Britain*. London: Penguin.

FOGELMAN, K.R. (1975) 'Developmental correlates of family size,' *British Journal of Social Work*, **5**, 1, 31–43.

FOGELMAN, K.R. and RICHARDSON, K. (1974) 'School attendance and results from the National Child Development Study.' In: TURNER, B. (ed.) *Truancy*. London: Hutchinson Educational.

FUNKENSTEIN, D.H. (1963) 'The masculine role, mathematics and quantitative attitudes,' *Diseases of the Nervous System*, **24**, April suppl.

GABRIEL, K.R. (1966) 'Simultaneous test procedures for multiple comparisons on categorical data,' *Journal of the American Statistical Association*, **61**, 1081–96.

GEORGE, V. and WILDING, P. (1972) *Motherless Families*. London: Routledge and Kegan Paul.

GOODE, W.J. (1964) *The Family*. Englewood Cliffs, N.J.: Prentice Hall.

GOODE, W.J. (1965) *Women in Divorce*. New York: Collier-Macmillan.

GREGORY, I. (1965) 'Anterospective data following childhood loss of a parent. (1) Delinquency and high school drop-out,' *Archives of General Psychiatry*, **13**, 2, 99–109.

GREVE, J., PAGE, D. and GREVE, S. (1971) *Homeless in London*. Edinburgh: Scottish Academic Press.

HANSEN, P. and HILL, B. (1964) 'Families under stress.' In: CHRISTENSEN, H.T. (ed.) *Handbook of Marriage and the Family*. Chicago: Rand McNally.

HERAUD, B.J. (1970) *Sociology and social work*. Oxford: Pergamon.

HERZOG, E. and SUDIA, C.E. (1968) 'Fatherless homes: a review of research,' *Children*, **15**, 5, 177–82.

HERZOG, E. and SUDIA, C.E. (1970) *Boys in Fatherless Families*. Washington, D.C.: US Dept. of Health, Education and Welfare.

HETHERINGTON, E.M. (1966) 'Effects of paternal absence on sex-typed behaviour in negro and white pre-adolescent males,' *Journal of Personality and Social Psychology*, **4**, 1, 87–91.

HITCHFIELD, E. *In Search of Promise*. London: Longman, in assoc. with National Children's Bureau.

HOLMAN, R. (1970) *Unsupported Mothers*. London: Mothers in Action.

HUNT, A. (1968) *A Survey of Women's Employment: a survey carried out on behalf of the Ministry of Labour by the Government Social Survey, 1965*. London: HMSO.

HUNT, A. *et al.* (1973) *Families and their Needs with particular reference to One-Parent Families.* London: HMSO.

KAY, S. (1971) 'Problems of accepting means-tested benefits.' In: BULL, D. (ed.) *Family Poverty: Programme for the Seventies.* London: Duckworth, in assoc. with Child Poverty Action Group.

KLEIN, V. (1965) *Britain's Married Women Workers.* London: Routledge and Kegan Paul.

KOCH, M.B. (1961) 'Anxiety in pre-school children from broken homes,' *Merrill-Palmer Quarterly*, 7, 4, 225—31.

KRIESBERG, L. (1967) 'Rearing children for educational achievement in fatherless families,' *Journal of Marriage and the Family*, 29, 288—301.

KRIESBERG, L. (1970) *Mothers in Poverty.* Chicago, Aldine.

LANIER, J.A. (1949) 'A guidance-faculty study of student withdrawals,' *Journal of Educational Research*, 43 3, 205—12.

LASLETT, P. (1972) *Household and family in past time.* Cambridge University Press.

LYNES, T. (1971) 'The failure of selectivity.' In: BULL. D. (ed.) *Family Poverty: Programme for the Seventies.* London: Duckworth, in assoc. with Child Poverty Action Group.

LYNN, D.B. and SAWREY, W.L. (1959) 'The effects of father absence on Norwegian boys and girls,' *Journal of Abnormal and Social Psychology*, 59, 2.

McCORD, J., McCORD, W. and THURBER, E. (1962) 'Some effects of paternal absence on male children,' *Journal of Abnormal and Social Psychology*, 64, 5, 361—9.

McKAY, A., GEORGE, V. and WILDING, P. (1972) 'Stereotypes of male and female roles and their influence on people's attitudes to one-parent families,' *Sociological Review*, 20, 1, 79—92.

MALMQUIST, E. (1958) 'Factors relating to reading disabilities in the first grade of the elementary school.' (Abstract) *Educational Research*, 1, 1, 69—72.

MAPSTONE, E. (1969) 'Children in care,' *Concern*, 3, 23—8. NCB.

MARRIS, P. (1958) *Widows and their Families.* London: Routledge and Kegan Paul.

MARSDEN, D. (1969) *Mothers Alone.* London: Allen Lane; Penguin Press.

MILLER, S.M., SALEEM, B., and BRYCE, H. (1964) *School Drop-Outs: a Commentary and Annotated Bibliography.* Syracuse, N.Y.: Syracuse Youth Development Center.

MINISTRY OF HOUSING AND LOCAL GOVERNMENT (1965) *Report of the Committee on Housing in Greater London.* London: HMSO. (Milner Holland report)

MINISTRY OF HOUSING AND LOCAL GOVERNMENT (1969) *Council Housing, Purposes, Procedures and Priorities*. London: HMSO. (Cullingworth report)

MINISTRY OF SOCIAL SECURITY (1967) *Circumstances of Families*. London: HMSO.

NASH, J. (1965) 'The father in contemporary culture and current psychological literature,' *Child Development*, **36**, 1, 261–97.

NEWSON, J. and NEWSON, E. (1970) 'Changes in the concept of parenthood.' In: ELLIOTT, K. (ed.) *The Family and its Future*. London: Churchill.

NYE, F.I. (1957) 'Child adjustment in broken or unhappy unbroken homes,' *Marriage and Family Living*, **19**, 356–61.

NYE, F.I. (1963) The adjustment of adolescent children. In: NYE, F.I., and HOFFMAN, L.W., *The Employed Mother in America*. Chicago: Rand McNally.

PACKMAN, J. (1968) *Child Care: Needs and Numbers*. London: Allen and Unwin.

PIDGEON, D.A. (1970) *Expectation and Pupil Performance*. Slough: NFER.

PILLING, D. (in press) *The Father's Role in the Family*.

PINDER, P. (1969) *Women at Work*. London: Political and Economic Planning.

PRINGLE, M.L. Kellmer, BUTLER, N.R., and DAVIE, R. (1966) *11,000 Seven Year Olds*. London: Longman in assoc. with National Children's Bureau.

REGISTRAR GENERAL'S OFFICE (1960) *Classification of Occupations*. London: HMSO.

ROSENBERG, M. (1965) *Society and the Adolescent Self-Image*. Princeton, NJ: Princeton University Press.

ROSENTHAL, R. and JACOBSON, L. (1968) *Pygmalion in the Classroom*. New York: Holt, Rinehart and Winston.

ROWNTREE, G. (1955) 'Early childhood in broken homes,' *Population Studies*, **8**, 247.

RUSSELL, I.L. (1957) 'Behaviour problems of children from broken and intact homes,' *Journal of Educational Sociology*, **31**, 124–29.

RUTTER, M. (1966) *Children of Sick Parents: an Environmental and Psychiatric Study*. London: Oxford University Press.

RUTTER, M. (1972) *Maternal Deprivation Re-assessed*. London: Penguin.

SANCTUARY, G. and WHITEHEAD, C. (1970) *Divorce – and After*. London: Gollancz.

SCHLESINGER, B. (1966) 'The one-parent family: an overview,' *Family Life Co-ordinator*, **15** 133–39.

SCHLESINGER, B. (1969) *The One-Parent Family: Perspectives and Annotated Bibliography*. Toronto, Ont.: Toronto University Press.

SEARS, P.S. (1951) 'Doll play aggression in normal young children: influence of sex, age, sibling status, father's absence,' *Psychological Monographs*, **65**, 6.

SEGLOW, J., PRINGLE, M.L. Kellmer, and WEDGE, P. (1972) *Growing Up Adopted*. Slough: NFER. (A National Children's Bureau report.)

SIEGEL, A.E., STOLZ, L.M. and ADAMSON, J. (1963) 'Dependence and independence in children.' In: NYE, F.I. and HOFFMAN, L.W. *The Employed Mother in America*. Chicago: Rand McNally.

SLATER, P.E. (1964) 'Parental role differentiation.' In: COSER, R.L. (ed.) *The Family: its Structure and Functions*. New York: St. Martins Press.

SPREY, J. (1969) 'The study of single parenthood: some methodological considerations.' In: SCHLESINGER, B. *The One-Parent Family: Perspectives and Annotated Bibliography*. Toronto, Ont.: Toronto University Press.

STOLZ, L.M. (1960) 'Effects of maternal employment on children: evidence from research,' *Child Development*, **31**, 749–82.

THOMES, M.M. (1968) 'Children with absent fathers,' *Journal of Marriage and the Family*, **30**, 1, 89–96.

TITMUSS, R.M. (1953) *The Family*. London: National Council of Social Service.

WALLENSTEIN, N. (1937) *Character and Personality of Children from Broken Homes*. New York: Teachers' College, Columbia University Press.

WALLSTON, B. (1973) 'The effects of maternal employment on children,' *Journal of Child Psychology and Psychiatry*, **14** 2, 81–95.

WEDGE, P. and PROSSER, H. (1973) *Born to Fail?* London: Arrow Books, in assoc. with National Children's Bureau.

WEST, D.J. (1969) *Present Conduct and Future Delinquency*. London: Heinemann.

WILSON, B. (1962) 'The teacher's role – a sociological analysis,' *British Journal of Sociology*, **13**, 1, 15–32.

WIMPERIS, V. (1960) *The Unmarried Mother and her Child*. London: Allen and Unwin.

WYNN, M. (1964) *Fatherless Families*. London: Michael Joseph.

YOUNG, M. and WILLMOTT, P. (1957) *Family and Kinship in East London*. London: Routledge and Kegan Paul.

YOUNG, M. and WILLMOTT, P. (1973) *The Symmetrical Family*. London: Routledge and Kegan Paul.

YUDKIN, S. and HOLME, A. (1963) *Working Mothers and their Children*. London: Michael Joseph.

INDEX

and father's aspiration for leaving age
98—9
and father's discussion with school
95—6
and father's interest 97
and father's unemployment 66—7
and free school meals 52
and health of father 144
and housing 71—82, 84
number of children 37, 39
and outings with father 101—2
and reading attainment 107—110,
117—8, 120, 147—8
and social adjustment 122—4, 128
and social class 41—2, 46
and social services contacts 87—9
and special schools 105
and Supplementary Benefit 50
definition of one-parent family 29—30
desertion — see marital breakdown
divorce — see marital breakdown

employment, mother's 58—69
and day care 59, 60, 63
and educational background 64
and effects on children 67—9, 111—
2, 115—6
and family size 63
attitudes to working mothers 58
full time 61—2, 63, 65
hours away from home 65—6
part-time 61—2, 63, 65
enuresis 19, 22, 128—30

family size 42—4
definition of, 42
financial position of one-parent children:
see Free School Meals, Supplementary
Benefit
Finer Report 28, 33, 48, 56, 70, 92
free school meals 51—3, 53—4, 56
take-up 53

Gingerbread 16
grandfather 35
grandmother 35

health of mother 143—4, 145
health of father 143—4, 145
homelessness — see housing
housing — amenities 74—6
bed sharing 78—9
effects on children 84—5
homelessness 84

local authority housing 72, 76
mobility 79—81
overcrowding 77—8
owner occupation 72—3
privately rented 73—4, 76, 78, 79,
80—1, 82—3
satisfaction with 82—3
type of accommodation

illegitimacy and
absence from school 141—2
age of mother 45—6
arithmetic attainment 114—6, 147
backwardness 105
children in care 91
children living away 44
children's aspirations for further
training 133—4
children's mention of marriage 137
enuresis 129
family size 42
feelings of hardship 54—5
free school meals 52, 56
health of mother 143
housing 71—83
mother working 61—5
mother's aspiration for leaving age 98
mother's aspiration for further training 99
mother's discussion with school 95
mother's interest 96—7
number of children 36, 38
outings with mother 100
reading attainment 110—12, 120,
147
social adjustment 124—5, 127—8
social class 41
social services contacts 87
Supplementary Benefit 50—1

marital breakdown — fatherless
and absence from school 141—2
and age of mother 45—6
and arithmetic attainment 112—6,
118—9, 147
and backwardness 105
and children in care 91
and children living away 44
and children's aspirations for further
training 133—4
and children's mention of marriage
137—8
and enuresis 128—9
and family size 42—3, 46